Cambridge Elements ☰

Elements in the Problems of God
edited by
Michael L. Peterson
Asbury Theological Seminary

THE PROBLEM OF GOD IN JEWISH THOUGHT

Jerome Gellman
Ben-Gurion University of the Negev

With

Joseph (Yossi) Turner
Schechter Institutes of Jewish Studies

T0323924

CAMBRIDGE
UNIVERSITY PRESS

Shaftesbury Road, Cambridge CB2 8EA, United Kingdom

One Liberty Plaza, 20th Floor, New York, NY 10006, USA

477 Williamstown Road, Port Melbourne, VIC 3207, Australia

314–321, 3rd Floor, Plot 3, Splendor Forum, Jasola District Centre, New Delhi – 110025, India

103 Penang Road, #05–06/07, Visioncrest Commercial, Singapore 238467

Cambridge University Press is part of Cambridge University Press & Assessment, a department of the University of Cambridge.

We share the University's mission to contribute to society through the pursuit of education, learning and research at the highest international levels of excellence.

www.cambridge.org
Information on this title: www.cambridge.org/9781009565158

DOI: 10.1017/9781009267113

First published 2024

A catalogue record for this publication is available from the British Library

ISBN 978-1-009-56515-8 Hardback
ISBN 978-1-009-26710-6 Paperback
ISSN 2754-8724 (online)
ISSN 2754-8716 (print)

Cambridge University Press & Assessment has no responsibility for the persistence or accuracy of URLs for external or third-party internet websites referred to in this publication and does not guarantee that any content on such websites is, or will remain, accurate or appropriate.

The Problem of God in Jewish Thought

Elements in the Problems of God

DOI: 10.1017/9781009267113
First published online: December 2024

Jerome Gellman
Ben-Gurion University of the Negev

With

Joseph (Yossi) Turner
Schechter Institutes of Jewish Studies

Author for correspondence: Jerome Gellman, gellman@bgu.ac.il

Abstract: The Hebrew Bible contains two quite different divine personae. One is quick to anger and to exact punishment while the other is a compassionate God slow to anger and quick to forgive. One God distant, the other close by. This severe contrast posed a theological challenge for Jewish thought for the ages. This Element follows selected views in rabbinic literature, medieval Jewish philosophy, Jewish mystical thought, the Hasidic movement, modern Jewish theology, response to the Holocaust, and Jewish feminist theology. In the history of Jewish thought there was often a tendency to identify closely with the God of compassion.

Keywords: two divine personae, judgment, compassion, medieval/modern thought, rabbinic literature

ISBNs: 9781009565158 (HB), 9781009267106 (PB), 9781009267113 (OC)
ISSNs: 2754-8724 (online), 2754-8716 (print)

Contents

1 The Two Faces of God: The Hebrew Bible

This study is about the two conflicting divine personae of the God of the Jews. I trace here how this duality fared in the thought of select Jewish thinkers and movements over history. My selection includes only those who thought of themselves as within the Jewish tradition or were wanting to revise that tradition sufficiently to be loyal to it. This includes a wide swath of thinkers and theologies. However, this leaves out some illustrious thinkers who were Jewish, such as Baruch Spinoza and Martin Buber. As well, other important thinkers will be left out because their thought is less relevant to this Element, and, alas, because this is a short Element.

1.1 The God of Exacting Punishment

The source of the two personae of the God of the Jews is in the Hebrew Bible. On the one hand, we find there a God who will get furiously angry, is slow to forgive; a God who serves out and delivers threats and horrific punishments for disobedience. In short, the proverbial "God of the Old Testament."

Here, see this God:

> I will bring upon you sudden terror, wasting diseases and fever that will destroy your sight and drain away your life . . . You will eat the flesh of your sons and the flesh of your daughters. I will . . . pile your dead bodies on the lifeless forms of your idols. I myself will lay waste the land, so that your enemies who live there will be appalled. I will scatter you among the nations and will draw out my sword and pursue you. Your land will be laid waste, and your cities will lie in ruins. (Leviticus 26:16–33)

And here:

> However, if you do not obey the LORD your God and do not carefully follow all his commands and decrees I am giving you today, all these curses will come on you and overtake you . . . . The Lord will send on you curses, confusion and rebuke in everything you put your hand to, until you are destroyed and come to sudden ruin because of the evil you have done in forsaking him. The Lord will plague you with diseases until he has destroyed you from the land you are entering to possess. The Lord will strike you with wasting disease, with fever and inflammation, with scorching heat and drought, with blight and mildew, which will plague you until you perish. (Deuteronomy 28:15, 20–21)

This God is quick to punish, without warning:

> And the people complained in the hearing of the LORD about their misfortunes; and when the LORD heard it, his anger was kindled, and the fire of the LORD burned among them, and consumed some outlying parts of the

camp. Then the people cried to Moses; and Moses prayed to the LORD, and the fire abated. (Numbers 11:1–2)

And once again in Numbers 16:42–49:

> When the assembly gathered in opposition to Moses and Aaron and turned toward the tent of meeting, suddenly the cloud covered it and the glory of the LORD appeared. Then Moses and Aaron went to the front of the tent of meeting, and the LORD said to Moses, "Get away from this assembly so I can put an end to them at once."

A plague begins without warning to the people. Then Aaron stops the plague by carrying incense through the Israelite camp. And so, "[Aaron] stood between the living and the dead, and the plague stopped. And 14,700 people died from the plague."

So, 14,700 people died from the plague, without warning or a chance to repent.

Think, as well, of when King David takes a census of all the tribes. The prophet Gad tells David of God's displeasure at the taking the census. And then: "The Lord sent a pestilence on Israel from that morning until the appointed time; and seventy thousands of the people died" (2 Samuel 24:15).

And famously, in Deuteronomy 20:16–18, Moses tells the Israelites:

> As for the towns of these peoples that the Lord your God is giving you as an inheritance, you must not let anything that breathes remain alive. You shall annihilate them – the Hittites and the Amorites, the Canaanites and the Perizzites, the Hivites and the Jebusites – just as the Lord your God has commanded.

Finally, from Lamentations 2:2–4, a punishment God visits on the people with "heated anger":

> God eradicated without compassion all of Jacob's pastures. He destroyed in his fury Daughter Judah's fortresses. He brought to the ground and profaned a kingdom and its princes. He cut down in fierce anger every horn of Israel. He held back his right arm in the face of the enemy. And He burned in Jacob like a fiery flame, consuming all around. He drew his bow like an enemy, His right hand steadied like a foe; And He slew every delight of the eye. Onto the tent of Daughter Zion He poured His venom like fire.

This is one divine persona, found throughout the Hebrew Bible.

1.2 The Compassionate God

The same God of the Jews of the Hebrew Bible is equally a thoroughly compassionate, loving God, slow to anger, and withholding of retribution. Take a look at another, contrasting, side of the God of the Jews: "Our ancestors became arrogant and stiff-necked, and they did not obey your commands . . . But you are a forgiving God, gracious and compassionate, slow to anger and abounding in love. Therefore, you did not desert them" (Neḥemiah 9:16–18) and, "For the Lord your God is a merciful God. He will not fail you, destroy you, or forget the covenant with your ancestors which he swore to them" (Deuteronomy 4:31). "And He [God] passed in front of Moses, proclaiming, "The LORD, the LORD, the compassionate and gracious God, slow to anger, abounding in love and faithfulness" (Exodus 34:6).

"And in Isaiah 54:10: "Though the mountains be shaken, and the hills be removed, yet my unfailing love for you will not be shaken nor my covenant of peace be removed," says the Lord, who has compassion on you."

And in Psalms 103:1–8

> Praise the LORD, O my soul, and forget not all his benefits, who forgives all your sins and heals all your diseases, who redeems your life from the pit and crowns you with love and compassion . . . The LORD works righteousness and justice for all the oppressed . . . The LORD is compassionate and gracious, slow to anger, abounding in love.

And, again, in Psalms 145:8–9 and 17: "The Lord is gracious and compassionate, slow to anger and rich in kindness. The Lord is good to all; he has compassion on all he has made . . . The LORD is righteous in all he does, merciful in all his acts."

And in Joel 2:13: "Return to the LORD your God, for he is gracious and compassionate, slow to anger and abounding in love, and he relents from sending calamity." Here, God is slow to anger, always compassionate and merciful, and forgiving of sins.

So, we have two configurations of the God of the Jews, portraying two severely opposed divine personae: the one slow to anger, always merciful and easily forgiving; the other virtually unforgiving, who rages in anger; the one wholly compassionate, and the one who punishes furiously at times without warning. These two personae cannot easily, if at all, be reconciled. The story of this Element tells of ways Jewish thinkers and movements have faced these strongly clashing dual personae of God.

2 The Rabbinic Literature I

I turn now to the rabbinic literature. Within this literature, the two divine personae find homes in two different divine names. Rabbinic literature spans a period roughly from the beginning of the Common Era to about 600 CE, from rabbis in Palestine and Babylon. It includes legal and non-legal teachings and comprises the Mishnah (completed in the third century), the Jerusalem Talmud (completed in the fifth century) and Babylonian Talmud (completed in the sixth century), and ancillary texts including the Toseftah and most of Midrash.

These contrasting features of the God of the Jews get named in the rabbinic literature as: *midat ha'rahamim*, the attribute of Compassion/Mercy, and *midat ha'din*, the attribute of severe Judgment. Now, the most common names of God in the Hebrew Bible are "YHWH" and "ELOHIM." (I set aside for our purposes biblical-critical understandings of these two names of God. That is because I am interested here in the historical reception of the names and the dual personae when dealing with the tradition. Critical views go in very different directions.) There is no uniform Rabbinic view on the import of these names, yet the most influential view in Jewish history was to identify "YHWH" with mercy and "ELOHIM" with judgment.

An early influential rabbinic text marks this correlation explicitly: "Wherever "YHWH" occurs it designates the attribute of mercy, *midat ha'rahamim* ... wherever "ELOHIM" occurs it designates the attribute of judgment, *midat ha'din*" (Sifre, Deuteronomy section 26).

And in a later text, by Rabbi Samuel (third–fourth century): Says Rabbi Samuel son of Nahman, "Wherever it says, 'YHWH' – it is the characteristic of mercy, *midat ha-rahamim* .... Wherever it says, 'ELOHIM' – it is *midat ha'din*, the characteristic of judgment" (Genesis Rabbah 33:8).

It is very difficult to make out those contrasting connotations for the two names in the Hebrew Bible. There seem to be quite a number of counterexamples. Despite the difficulties in making that correlation between the names and the attributes of God, this matchup became quite standard with traditional biblical commentators and Jewish thinkers, at least until modern times.

I note that there are yet two important differences – although not systematic – between the names in the Torah that might have led the rabbis to want to make this distinction between YHWH and ELOHIM. The first is that YHWH *tends* to be more anthropomorphic than ELOHIM, although ELOHIM does not escape such description. (For a study of the name YHWH see: Ben-Sasson and Halbertal, 2012, 53–69 and Ben-Sasson, 2018.) ELOHIM appears in Genesis 1 as the transcendent creator of the world. "YHWH" is added to "ELOHIM" starting in Genesis 2, when God is hands-on inside the world and when God creates Adam from the soil and places him in the Garden of Eden.

A "powerful hand" and "outstretched arm" that save and protect the Israelites, are typically of YHWH. It is YHWH who commands to make a place for him on earth, to be close to the Israelites in the desert Sanctuary: "And YHWH spoke to Moses saying, ... They shall make for me a sanctuary, that I may dwell among them" (Exodus 25:1,8). And subsequently it is YHWH who commands the details of the holy sanctuary. It is YHWH who smells the good fragrance of the sacrifices in the Sanctuary (Leviticus 1:9). These are indications of YHWH's closeness to the people to which the rabbis might have paid special attention in seeing YHWH as *midat ha-raḥamim*, the attribute of mercy.

A typical way for ELOHIM to communicate is through dreams, which are considered a message from *beyond*. For example, the command to Abraham to sacrifice his son is said in a dream by ELOHIM. Then Abraham arises the next morning to carry out the deed (Genesis 22:3). This places ELOHIM further away from us than is YHWH, who typically communicates directly or through an angel of YHWH present here on earth. And it is an angel of YHWH who stays Abraham's hand when he is about to kill his son Isaac.

There is a second difference between the names "ELOHIM" and "YHWH" that would have made the matching between the names and the attributes seem natural. "ELOHIM" is not a proper name of God, but a common noun. It is the plural of "eloha," meaning simply "a god," small "g." "YHWH" is the proper name of the God of the Jews, like "John" and "Jane." Appropriately, as we have seen, ELOHIM in the Torah *tends* to be more abstract, transcendent, less anthropomorphic than YHWH. "ELOHIM" when used of God is really more of a title, like "the Prime Minister," than a name of God.

"ELOHIM" also connotes judges. The word "ELOHIM" refers to human judges, as in Exodus 22:8, according to Jewish tradition and in standard English translations: "But if the thief is not found, the owner of the house must appear before the ELOHIM [Judges], and they must determine whether the owner of the house has laid hands on the other person's property."

On the other hand, "YHWH" is a personal, proper name of God. Appropriately, it conveys the way the Israelites experience their God. It is their name for their God. A name others might not recognize. So, in Exodus 5:2, we find: "And Pharaoh said, 'who is YHWH that I should obey his voice to let Israel go? I know not YHWH, neither will I let Israel go.'" This God *tends* to be more anthropomorphic than ELOHIM, hence more personal than ELOHIM, and appears more readily, and *tends* to be more comforting.

It is YHWH who says to the Israelites, "Although the whole earth is mine, you will be for me a kingdom of priests and a holy nation" (Exodus 19:5–6). And it is YHWH who says to them, "You are the children of YHWH your God . . . Out of all the peoples on the face of the earth, YHWH has chosen you to be his treasured possession." So, it would have been natural to slide from such verses to identify YHWH with the attribute of Mercy, and ELOHIM otherwise. However, as I have already said, the difference between YHWH and ELOHIM across the board is difficult to make out with any consistency.

It will be convenient to have two names handy for the two divine personae, *irrespective of how they may be named in the Hebrew Bible*. In a gesture to what became a dominant view, that "ELOHIM" connotes severe judgment and "YHWH" compassion, the two names will be "PERSONA-Y" and "PERSONA-E," for "Divine Persona-YHWH" and "Divine Persona-ELOHIM." (Again, this choice reflects no agreement to the systematic occurrence of the names "ELOHIM" and "YHWH" in the Hebrew Bible. These are no more than convenient names.)

The names "PERSONA-Y" and "PERSONA-E," respectively, are to denote different *clusters* of semantic fields, the Y-cluster and the E-cluster. The *ruling idea* of the Y-cluster will be that PERSONA-Y is the divine persona *close* to us, both in presence and in intimacy. *Accordingly,* Cluster-Y will include the following (and related ideas) under its ruling idea – that PERSONA-Y is accessible, present, and intimate to a significant degree; that PERSONA-Y is benevolent, merciful, loving, and forgiving; that PERSONA-Y is best understood in anthropomorphic terms; above all, PERSONA-Y is deserving of our love. This is the God of the Israelites/Jews more than of the non-Jews.

The *ruling idea* of the E-cluster will be that this divine persona is *distant* from us. *Accordingly,* Cluster-E will include the following (and related ideas) under its ruling idea – that PERSONA-E tends to be abstract and transcendent (less-anthropomorphic) to a significant degree; that PERSONA-E is the majestic creator and ruler of the universe; that PERSONA-E is the source of natural, moral, and religious law; that PERSONA-E is the demanding, supreme judge; that PERSONA-E is "slow to forgive"; that PERSONA-E is deserving of fear and awe, and is given at times to severe anger and punishment. This is the God of absolute power, the God outside the world as creator, the judge sitting high in the court of justice, the judge who sentences in accordance with impersonal law.

In what follows, when this book says of a movement or thinker that they "favor" or "tend" to one divine persona over another, please keep in mind that:

(1) They need not endorse the entire related cluster of divine features of PERSONA-E or PERSONA-Y but need endorse only *enough* of the one cluster so that their God be closer to one persona rather than another.
(2) There may be elements of the other cluster in their thinking, but these will be few and/or play a secondary role.
(3) They need not have thought in terms of the two divine personae at all. Rather, this can be what will emerge for us, from their thought, as we assess the relevance to our topic.

3 The Rabbinic Literature II

In rabbinic literature we find one, influential, strand that raises up the God of love and compassion. Rabbinic literature is composed mostly of conversations and disagreements between many rabbis, with a panoply of views on just about everything. (Very Jewish!) There are wide differences in theologies within and between the early Mishnah and the ensuing Talmudic literature. Hence, there is nothing like *the* rabbinic view of the relationship between God's Mercy and Judgment (see Urbach, 1975, chapter 15). Nonetheless, the rabbinic literature displays a grand effort by many rabbis of different generations to soften the attribute of Justice and highlight the God of love and mercy. Rabbinic literature is marked by extreme anthropomorphism, even more than the Hebrew Bible. And this often contributes to a depiction of God as close to us, rather like us, as is befitting to PERSONA-Y.

The move by various rabbis of the Talmud to put PERSONA-Y in the center and weaken PERSONA-E is well illustrated, quite surprisingly, by the Talmudic concept of "suffering from love." Here, in a conceptual revolution, God is said at times to send suffering from God's *love* of a person.

> Raba (some say, R. Ḥisda) says: If a man sees that painful sufferings visit him, let him examine his conduct. For it is said: Let us search and try our ways and return unto the Lord (Lamentations 3:40). If he examines and finds nothing [objectionable] . . . let him be sure that these are chastenings of love. Raba, in the name of R. Saḥorah, in the name of R. Huna, says: If the Holy One, blessed be He, is pleased with a man, he crushes him with painful sufferings. For it is said: And the Lord was pleased with [him, hence] he crushed him by disease (Isaiah 53:10). The sufferings must be endured with consent. (Talmud, Berakhot 5a)

Here a type of suffering is transferred from the hands of punishment and Judgment to the God of love. Paradoxically, the God of love will visit suffering on the innocent for good purposes. This includes visiting suffering on the saintly so as to reward them, in this life or the next, for accepting the suffering with equanimity, aye, with love.

There was even a rabbinic belief that human suffering was the greatest of gifts from God to us. Rabbi Akiva (*c*.50?–*c*.135? CE) and his followers blunted the distinction between Mercy and Judgment, by joyfully welcoming suffering. R. Akiva died happily when the Romans murdered him, with R. Akiva thanking God for having him die as a martyr. And R. Akiva was the first to call God by the name, "Raḥmana," ("Merciful") and it is he who said that "suffering is beloved" (Talmud, Sanhedrin: 101a). R. Akiva is assumed the author of the saying, "If I bring upon you good, give thanks and if I bring you suffering, give thanks."

Suffering can be good because it purifies a person. So, R. Akiva said this: "Happy are you the people of Israel, for before whom are you purified and who purifies you? Your Father in Heaven . . . Just as a ritual bath purifies the ritually impure, just so the Blessed Holy One purifies the people, Israel" (Mishnah Yoma 8:9).

For R. Akiva, one of the ways God purifies is by bringing suffering upon a person. To become purified in a ritual bath you must be entirely immersed in the water. Just so, suffering "immerses" a person into misery and thus will purify them. God purifies with suffering much as the ritual bath does with water.

And it was R. Akiva, distancing from PERSONA-E, who said that all books of the Bible were holy, but that the Song of Songs (Canticles), a love story, was the "holy of the holies," a reference to the holiest precinct of the Jerusalem Temple. This same rabbi who cherished suffering lauded the God of love.

Other voices in the rabbinic literature labor to diminish Persona-E as a face of God, by portraying God as strongly allied with Mercy, even to the point of treating God as though having *only* PERSONA-Y. The attribute of judgment is thought of as virtually external to God and threatening of God's Mercy. The Babylonian Talmud has this striking passage:

> Rabbi Yoḥanan said in the name of Rabbi Yosei: How do we know that the Holy One, Blessed be He, prays? For it says: "I will bring them to My holy mountain and make them joyful in the house of my prayer" (Isaiah 56:7). It does not say the house of *their* prayer, but "the house of *my* prayer"; from this we know that the Holy One, Blessed be He, prays. What does God pray?? Rav Zutra bar Tovia said that Rav said: God says: "May it be my will that my mercy will defeat my anger towards Israel for their sins, and may my mercy overcome my other attributes through which I punish Israel. And may I act toward My children, Israel, with the attribute of mercy, and may I act beyond the letter of the law." (Berakhot 7a)

Here is God wanting to act only from Mercy. But God is apprehensive of Judgment interfering, as though Judgment were a force external to God. So, God prays for the strength to withstand the power of the adversary to His Mercy. To whom does God pray? To God.

The Talmud continues on to record that God once asked the High Priest of the Temple, Yishmael ben Elisha, to pray for God's sake. The high priest prays the same prayer that God prays, that the divine Mercy overcome Judgment. God then "nods his head and accepts the prayer." Here God asks for help to gain the strength to persevere on behalf of embracing Mercy.

There are many rabbinic passages in which God must engage in trickery to prevent the attribute of Judgment from foiling divine intentions. In the following, the attribute of Judgment appears as a threatening force, independent of God: "Rabbi Ḥanina said that when God came to create Adam, the angels asked what sort of being this would be. God answered simply, "Righteous people will be his descendants."

The Rabbi goes on to say: "God revealed to them [only] that the righteous will descend from Adam. For had he revealed to them that evil people will also descend from Adam, the attribute of Judgment would not have let God create Adam" (Bereshit Rabbah, Section Bereshit, 8).

God must keep it a secret that evil people will descend from Adam, lest Judgment find out and defeat God's plans. Here God is virtually identical only with PERSONA-Y.

In the following, Satan personifies judgment, furthering judgment yet more disconnected from God. The scene takes place on Yom Kippur, the holy day of fasting and praying for God's forgiveness for our sins:

> On Yom Kippur comes Satan to prosecute the Jewish people. He details their sins [before God] . . . Then the Blessed Holy One details their merits. What does God then do? He takes a rod of a scale and weighs [on pans] the sins against the merits. And they are balanced. So, Satan goes out to bring more sins to put on the pan of the sins to decide the issue. What does the Blessed Holy One then do? Before Satan returns and wishes to add sins to the scale, the Blessed Holy One removes the sins from the pan and hides them under his royal robe. Then Satan returns and finds no sins. (Pesikta Rabbati 45)

God must outwit Judgment, personified by a being separate to and antagonistic toward God, to grant clemency on this holy day. God does that by removing the sins from the scale and then hiding them under his robe where Satan dare not look for them. God can then pretend that there were no sins there and proceed freely to grant forgiveness.

The verse in Psalms 91 where God says, "I am with him in his anguish," was widely interpreted to apply to the Israelite nation (as well as to individuals) and to be asserting that God himself suffers together with the people. So, for example, a rabbinic text says that when God freed the Israelites from Egypt, God was freeing himself since he suffered with their suffering (Shmot Rabbah 30;24).

God says that he will redeem the people from Egypt even if they do not deserve it, because God wishes to extricate *himself* from Egypt. God too is suffering there, and God's suffering must be imagined to be infinitely greater than humanity's. That was why, because the Israelites were then suffering in Egypt, that God appeared to Moses from a burning bush. God was suffering as though he himself was being burned in Egypt. According to a rabbinic text, God said to Moses at the burning bush: "Don't you feel that I am suffering as much as the Israelites are suffering? Know that from my speaking to you from the thorns I am as a partner in your suffering" (Shmot Rabbah 2:7).

This God of the Jews weeps. Jeremiah (8:23) says: "Would that my head were water, and my eye a fount of tears, that I might cry by day and night over the victims of the Daughter of My People!"

On this a rabbinic Midrash comments (Eikhah Rabbah 1:1): "Who must have said this verse? If you say it was Jeremiah, could he do without eating? Could he do without sleeping? Rather, who must have said this verse is one for whom there is no eating and no sleeping, as it is written (Psalms 121:4): "The Guardian of Israel never slumbers and never sleeps."

One crying all day and all night, could not sleep or eat. Hence, this biblical verse must have been said by God who needs no food or sleep. God cries in sorrow for God's suffering people. This is the God of Mercy.

This next example also pictures God as vulnerable to the attribute of Judgment. It pertains to the wicked king of Judah, Menashe, who repents of his sins and God forgives him. This was when Menashe was captured and taken to Babylon. As it is written, "In his distress [Menashe] sought the favor of his God and humbled himself greatly before the God of his ancestors. And when he prayed to him, God was moved by his entreaty and listened to his plea; so, he brought him back to Jerusalem and to his kingdom." (Chronicles 2 33:13–14).

The following from the Jerusalem Talmud depends on an alternative version of these verses, which reads (in translation), God "dug for him," in place of "God was moved by his entreaty." God digs for Menashe. What does it mean that God digs?

> The ministering angels said to God, "Master of the universe, a person who worshipped idols and placed an idol in the Temple, you are going to accept his repentance?!" God said to them, "If I do not accept his repentance, I will be locking the door before all who repent." What did God do? He dug for [Menashe] an "underground" path to his royal throne and listened to his supplications.

The angels are right. Menashe is too evil to be forgiven, according to the attribute of Justice. So, God must find a way to forgive Menashe against the angels who give voice to Judgment. It appears that God cannot stand up directly against this voice. So, God must forgive Menashe secretly so that the angels will not know. God finds a way to outfox Judgment and pour his Mercy on the repentant king. God digs a hidden "tunnel" for Menashe's prayers, so that will bypass Judgment. Then the God of Mercy triumphs.

There is even a quarrel between God and Justice, in which God loses the argument. This being the only time that such a thing happened, according to the Talmud. Here too, the attribute of Justice is personified as exterior to God. This takes us to Ezekiel 9, where the people who worshipped idols are all killed, while those who bewailed idol worship were saved. The Babylonian Talmud tells this story: "Said the Attribute of Justice before the Holy One, "blessed be He: Sovereign of the Universe! Wherein are these different from those?" Justice wanted them all to be killed. To which God replies: "Those are completely righteous, while these are completely wicked." "Those who are to be spared," responds God, "never worshipped idols while those to be killed did." Justice continued: "Sovereign of the Universe! [Those to be spared] had the power to reproach but did not."

Those people only bemoaned the state of sin in their midst, but did not actually confront the sinners with rebuke. Hence, they share in the sins of Jerusalem for not reproaching and they too should be killed. To this God replies: "It was fully known to them that had they protested, [the sinners] would not have heeded them." Justice responded: "Sovereign of the Universe! If it was revealed to Thee, was it revealed to them?"

God had no answer. Those he wished to spare had no idea that had they protested, in any case they would not have influenced the sinners for the good. In face of this, God must now reluctantly decree that even those who did not sin with idol worship must die, with the exception of those who had reproached the sinners. God had done his best and lost.

Worth mentioning here is another important strand of rabbinic thinking. This portrays God as needing the Jewish people as much as they need God (see Heschel, 2021, Volume 1, chapter 5.). This includes having God say to the Israelite nation, "The two of us need each other." According to this way of thinking, the Israelite people can weaken or increase the power of God: "So long as the righteous do the will of God they increase the power [of God]. But if not, it is written "You have weakened the Rock who has given birth to you" (Deuteronomy 32:18)

This strand of rabbinic thinking deflates the autonomous power of God and brings God into a close, mutual relationship with us; of God needing us as we need God. This goes well with that sector of rabbinic thought that tries to further God from the persona of E and closer to the persona of Y.

In all, we see within these significant strands of rabbinic writings a strong pull toward portraying God as allied with or even wholly identical with PERSONA-Y. In this strand, Judgment tends to become portrayed as separate from and antagonistic to the God of Mercy. And the God who has infinite power over us is compromised by God's own need of us. In this way the biblical duality within God becomes softened by replacing it with a cosmic collision between God and a personified demand for exacting punishment.

4 Medieval Jewish Philosophy

Medieval Jewish philosophy was heavily influenced by ancient Greek philosophy and by contemporary Muslim philosophers. Here, we look first at two of the great Jewish medieval figures, Saadia (or "Saadya") ben Joseph (882–942 CE) ("Saadia Gaon") and Moses Maimonides (1138–1204 CE). A major aim of these philosophers was to eliminate anthropomorphism of God. This resulted, in the case of Saadia, in favoring some of the key components of the E-cluster, thus moving the dial closer to PERSONA-E, while retaining the divine love and benevolence of PERSONA-Y. In the case of Maimonides, it was more of a *lurch* in the direction of PERSONA-E, including abstract transcendence and the source of a law-like world, with a rather abstract thinness to God's love and compassion, but without the anger and the fury.

There was a major objection to and retreat from this movement in philosophy, in the person of Judah Halevi (1075–1141 CE). He rejected "the God of the philosophers" in favor of "the God of Abraham, Isaac, and Jacob," long before Blaise Pascal (1623–1662 CE) wrote in favor of the "God of Abraham, God of Isaac, God of Jacob, not of the philosophers and the scholars." Halevi preceded Maimonides in time. However, Halevi's thought is best seen as a rejoinder to both Saadia's and Maimonides' *way* of favoring features of PERSONA-E at the expense of PERSONA-Y. So, I will be going out of chronological order here to present both Saadia and Maimonides before I turn to Halevi.

4.1 Saadia ben Joseph

The most highly regarded systematic Jewish philosopher of the early Middle Ages was Saadia ben Joseph (882–942). Saadia leaned strongly to some core elements of cluster-E, while still preserving some elements of PERSONA-Y. Saadia was born in Egypt and lived for some time in Palestine. He ended up in Babylon (today's Iraq), where he served as head of one of the Talmudic academies, in Sura. In practice, Saadia became the spiritual head of many of the Jewish people of the time.

Early on in his *The Book of Beliefs and Opinions* Saadia rejects the tradition that "YHWH" and "ELOHIM" connote a disparate bundle of attributes. "Scripture makes it clear that they both ["YHWH" and "ELOHIM"] have one connotation . . . no attention is to be paid to the fact that that one of the two appellatives is used in the description of one action while the other is used in describing another" (Saadia Gaon, 1948, 99.).

In his writings, Saadia often follows the Muslim, scholastic Kalam philosophers, both in style and content, and polemicizes strongly against the Karaites, and also against Christianity. The Karaites were Jews, flourishing in Saadia's time and later, who rejected the literature of the rabbinic period in favor of "Scripture alone." (See Lasker, 2022).

Saadia was determined to purify Judaism of anthropomorphism, associated heavily with PERSONA-Y in Judaism. He writes: "For all divine attributes pertaining to either substance or accident that are encountered in the books of the prophets it is necessary to find language of scripture nonanthropomorphic meanings that would be in keeping with the requirements of reason" (Saadia Gaon, 1948. 111–112.).

Here Saadia moves away from the more anthropomorphic of the two personae of God in the Bible, and the excessive anthropomorphic literature in the rabbinic age, toward the relative distance of PERSONA-E.

For Saadia, there are four sources of knowledge: that gained by direct observation; that gained by the intuition of the intellect; knowledge which is inferred by logical necessity, and finally, what he calls, depending on translation, "authentic" or "reliable," tradition. The latter includes testimony from others, especially from previous generations, including the Jewish tradition. It turns out that for Saadia the Jewish tradition itself must pass the bar of reason and must be validated. (This contention is controversial. Here I follow, among others, Abraham Joshua Heschel, 1944, 309–312). So, Saadia provides evidence for the historical truth of revelation at Sinai (Saadia Gaon, 1948, 30).

For Saadia, proofs of reason lead to knowledge that God created the world from nothing, that God is incorporeal and unchanging, and outside of time. So, God could not have human emotions of love, hate, anger, or grace, or pleasure. It follows that an authentic tradition could not have an anthropomorphic God.

Thus, Saadia has devoted himself to the eclipse of some of the Y-cluster, of God's intimate relationship with humans, especially with the Jews, of the God envisioned in human terms. Even the revelation to the Israelites at Mt. Sinai had to be given a support in reason. The primacy of reason moves the dial away from particularistic experiences of the Jewish people to universal validity for all nations. Saadia, in keeping with an emphasis on central features of PERSONA-E, the God of creation and ruler of the entire cosmos, shies away from a doctrine of the Jews as God's special possession:

> As regards the matter of possession, inasmuch as all creatures are God's creation and handiwork, it is not seemly for us to say that he possesses one thing to the exclusion of another, nor that he possesses the one to a greater and the other to a lesser degree. If we, nevertheless, see Scripture assert that a certain people is his peculiar property and his possession and his portion, as they do in the statement, "for the portion of the lord is his people, Jacob the lot of his inheritance" [Deut. 32:9], that is done merely as a means of conferring honor and distinction. For, as it appears to us, every man's portion and lot are precious to him. Nay the scriptures even go so far as to declare God, too, figuratively to be the lot of the pious and their portion, as they do in their statement, "Oh lord, the portion of mine inheritance and of my cup" [Psalms 16:5]. This is, therefore, also an expression of special devotion and esteem.

> It is also in this sense that one must construe the designation of God as the
> master of the prophets and of [all] believers, as he is called in such expres-
> sions used by scripture as the God of Abraham, the God of Isaac and the God
> of Jacob (Exodus 3:6), and the God of the Hebrews (Exodus 3:18). Such
> a designation is entirely in order since God is the master of all. This [special
> attachment of God's name] to the pious is, then, merely an expression of his
> esteem and high regard for them. (Saadia Gaon, 126).

God seems to have no special theologically based relationship to the Jews in
Saadia's philosophy. Saadia argues for accepting as rational the revelation at
Mt. Sinai but does not explain the particularism that shouts from this event.
Why the Jews and not all of humankind?

For Saadia, wishing to protect God's transcendence, a created reality, God's
"glory," not God's self, is what appears to prophets; God does not speak, but
modulated compressions of air can create human-like speech; and Saadia natural-
izes miracles as much as possible. Thus, for example, in the biblical story of Balaam
journeying to curse the Israelites in the desert. At one point, Balaam whips his
donkey for abruptly stopping on the way, and the donkey opens its mouth and
speaks words of protest to Balaam (Numbers 22: 28–30). Then Balaam sees an
angel of God who is blocking the donkey. In his naturalizing of apparent miracles as
much as possible, Saadia says that the donkey never spoke. All along it was the
angel, a created being, who was speaking, instead. This to preserve, as much as
possible, the rational order of the world created by the God of cosmic order.

You will find much about reward and punishment in Saadia's writings. And of
course, for Saadia God can be said to do acts of mercy and kindness. One of these
is God creating us for the purpose of human happiness. Another is revealing the
Torah. A third is God visiting suffering for the purpose of greater reward in the
afterlife. (See Stump, 1997). But such acts are not literally merciful, or from
anger, in God's really having thoughts or emotions of anger or mercy. God is not
like a person. God is out of time and unchanging, highly abstract and, as it were,
far away from us, even in revelational moments. *In this respect*, Saadia privileges
a transcendent PERSONA-E over PERSONA-Y, but without the anger and fury
of PERSONA-E that is not to be found in a non-anthropomorphic God. This is
a partial privileging of PERSONA-E that comes to its classic formulation in the
works of the greatest Medieval Jewish philosopher, Moses Maimonides.

4.2 Moses Maimonides

If I were to proceed chronologically, I would turn now to the most important
contra to the privileging of key elements of PERSONA-E in the Middle Ages.
This was in the person of Judah Halevi (c. 1075–1141), a Spanish Jew noted for
his Hebrew poetry and his philosophical treatise, *The Book of Refutation and*

Proof on Behalf of the Despised Religion. Instead, I choose to go out of chrono-logical order to first present the problem of God in the writings of Moses, son of Maimon, Maimonides (1138–1204), who was the greatest Jewish philosopher of the Middle Ages, and arguably of all times. Aquinas quotes Maimonides several times as "Rabbi Moses." I make this change of order because the critique of Halevi of "the God of the philosophers" and his defense of "the God of Abraham, Isaac, and Jacob" applies perfectly, and then some, to Maimonides who came after Halevi chronologically. It will be useful to see Halevi responding, as it were, to Maimonides' *type* of philosophy, if not to the person Maimonides, as well as to Saadia and others. So, I turn now to the "Great Eagle," as Maimonides has been called. After, I will turn to Judah Halevi.

Maimonides was born in Cordoba, Spain. When he was still a child, Cordoba was conquered by Berber Muslims who proceeded to set out to forcibly convert Jews to Islam. The family left Cordoba and went to Fez, Morocco. From 1171 Maimonides resided in Egypt, where he spent the rest of his life. Maimonides was the leader of the Egyptian Jews, and in effect the spiritual head of the Jewish people in his times. He also served as a physician in the court of the Sultan, Saladin. Maimonides wrote a massive and exhaust-ive work of Jewish law, *Mishneh Torah*, a book of logic, a series of medical books, various epistles to Jewish communities of his day, a commentary to the Mishnah of the rabbinic literature, legal decisions, and his philosophical magnum opus, *A Guide of The Perplexed*. After his death, Jews coined the phrase about the biblical Moses and Moses Maimonides, "From Moses to Moses there arose none like Moses." Such was and remains the esteem of Maimonides among the Jewish people.

Maimonides' *Guide* was written for the philosophically informed who were perplexed by the Hebrew Bible and rabbinic literature, principally by the anthropomorphism found there. In grand terms, Maimonides' aim was to reinterpret the Jewish tradition to conform as much as possible with his philo-sophical convictions. These latter were mainly derived from Aristotle, through Arabic translations and Muslim commentaries on *the* philosopher, and through some Muslim philosophers, especially al-Farabi (870?–951).

Two issues face us when trying to pin-down Maimonides' philosophical views. One is that the *Guide* is nothing even remotely resembling, for example, Aquinas' majestic philosophical edifices of his *Summas*. Maimonides was concerned to conceal some of his true views, largely to keep these from the unsophisticated for whom they would be difficult to accept or understand. In the introduction to the *Guide*, Maimonides tells the reader that the book contains contradictions between different passages, and it would be up to the perceptive reader to discern his true views. A topic could be advanced by opaque references and inconsistencies. These throw the reader off the trail, so as to give up Maimonides' true views only to those clever enough to fathom them.

The second issue is that in his other writings Maimonides at times takes positions more in keeping with popular views of the day. In his legal book, *Mishneh Torah*, he begins with an elaborate theological introduction and will add, when appropriate, theological reflections on laws. However, much of that work is in contrast to what Maimonides writes in the *Guide*. This has led some to posit two levels of Maimonides' thought: one exoteric and one esoteric. The exoteric level would conform much more than the esoteric to traditional Jewish thinking. The esoteric would conform more closely to Aristotle and to some of the Islamic philosophers.

These complications have resulted in a variety of ways of understanding Maimonides' philosophy. As one contemporary scholar once quipped, "there is my-monides, your-monides, his-monides, and her-monides." There are so many elements and disparities that trying to come up with a clear and consistent understanding is more difficult than solving a Rubik's cube. Many have earned a Ph.D. and professorship by joining the ongoing industry of trying to get the real Moses Maimonides to stand up. Here, I obviously cannot report on controversies over his views, and perforce what you will be reading will be my-monides, which is their-monides of others as well. This Maimonides embraces wholly, or nearly so, the God of the philosophers with rigor and ingenuity to place this God into the Jewish tradition.

The God of Maimonides is in the main a distant, universal God, the ground of all existence from whom flows a rational order for the entire universe, the sustainer of the world (and, possibly, the creator. See later). The God of Maimonides pretty much collapses into cluster-E, but without the anger and the fury.

The original basis of the Jewish religion, for Maimonides, was not an experience of God, or a revelation, but philosophy. For Maimonides, Abraham, the founder of the religion, came to know of God's existence by philosophical arguments. He then persuaded others of the existence of God by those same arguments. Here is Maimonides' description of Abraham as a philosopher:

> No sooner was this hero weaned than he began to ponder: "How can the sphere forever follow its course with none to conduct it? Who causes it to rotate? For it cannot possibly cause itself to rotate?" He had no one to teach or instruct him in anything ... while his mind was searching and seeking to understand – till he grasped the true way and understood the right course of his own sound reason: he realized that: there is a single God, he conducts the sphere, he created the universe, and, in all that exists, there is no God but he. And he realized that all the people were in error. (Maimonides, *Mishneh Torah*, Laws of Idolatry, 1:2–3)

The "sphere" here is the outermost sphere of medieval cosmology, which turns incessantly, moving the inner spheres, eventually giving to motion on earth. The inner spheres are moved by this outermost sphere, but what moves the outermost sphere? Abraham reasoned to the existence of God – the unmoved ultimate mover.

Maimonides goes on to say that Abraham then went about overcoming idol worshippers with his proofs: "Abraham triumphed over them with his arguments ... When people would gather to him and ask him about his words, he would teach each person in accordance with their intellect" (Maimonides, *Mishneh Torah*, Laws of Idolatry, 1:3).

And in another formulation about Abraham:

> When the pillar of the world grew up and it became clear to him that there is a separate deity that is neither a body nor a force in a body and that all the stars and the spheres were made by him, and he understood that the fables upon which he was brought up were absurd, he began to refute their doctrine and show up their opinions as false. (Maimonides, 1963, 3:29)

Quite at odds with the biblical account where Abraham knows of God for the first time when God calls Abraham to leave his home for Canaan, for Maimonides, Abraham kept moving about to defeat idolatry, "until he arrived at the land of Canaan." "God spoke to Abraham" gets parsed by Maimonides as "Abraham came to known that God exists by philosophical reasoning."

According to this scenario, Abraham discovered God intellectually, on his own. God did not choose Abraham, God did not seek him out, God did not make himself known to Abraham. There was no divine disclosure from the outside, as it were, to Abraham. On this Maimonidean understanding, God, as it were, waited till someone discovered him. God is entirely absent from this account of Maimonides as anything but the object of philosophical speculation. According to this account, God does not literally issue a command to Abraham to travel to Canaan.

This has implications not only for the primacy of philosophy, but for Maimonides' view of the Jews being the "chosen people." For given the understanding of Abraham as coming to know of God philosophically on his own, without divine help, it follows, as Matanel Bareli and Menachem Kellner write, that it just happened that Abraham was the one:

> That someone, happened to be Abraham, progenitor of the Jews. It did not have to be Abraham. Had the first human being to discover the truth about God been, say, a Navajo, and had that Navajo philosopher possessed the courage and effectiveness of Abraham, then the Navajos would be the chosen people, the Torah would have been composed in the Navajo language, its narratives would reflect their history, and many of its commandments would

reflect that history and the nature of Navajo society at the time of the giving of the Torah to them. The inner meaning of the Torah, its philosophical content, and spiritual message would all be equivalent to the inner meaning, philosophical content, and spiritual message of the Torah as it was indeed revealed to Moses at Sinai, but its outer garment would be dramatically different. (Bareli and Kellner, 2021: 144–145.)

Maimonides rarely, if ever, writes of the "chosenness" of the Jews and gives several indications of a universalistic attitude.

Moses was the greatest of the prophets. For Maimonides, prophecy was achieved by coming to such a high state of theological and scientific understanding that the prophet was able to tap into an intellectual emanation from the "active intellect." The "active intellect" is the last in the hierarchy of non-physical, "separate intellects," far superior to the human intellect. In the *Guide,* 2:36, Maimonides describes prophecy as an "overflow" from the active intellect, first to a person's rational faculty and then to the imaginative faculty. Moses reached the highest clarity of intellectual prophecy with a most developed imaginative faculty for knowing how to apply the prophetic content to legislation for a national existence. For Maimonides, God is only the distant cause of prophecy, by sustaining the structure of the world, including its scaffolding of the separate intellects, one of which is touched by the prophet directly.

The themes of philosophical attainment of prophecy and the effective downgrading of Jewish chosenness, raise the ruling idea of cluster-E of God's attributes to the forefront of Maimonides' philosophy. Which brings us to the core of Maimonides' thinking, his philosophy of God.

In his *Guide*, Maimonides devotes more than 60 chapters to debunking anthropomorphism, this being most likely the most attention given to undoing anthropomorphism in the medieval ages. God is not corporeal and is beyond human comprehension. God is simple in the most absolute sense. God has no inner composition, so that the multiplicity of attributes we assign to God does not exist in God but are descriptions of God's actions. Just as fire melts, cooks, burns, heats, and gives light, all from the one indivisible nature of fire, so does God act in a myriad of ways from God's one indivisible essence.

The only descriptions we can give of God himself are negative ones. We can say what God is not, but not what God is. God is not weak, not ignorant, and not evil. In truth, we could also say that God is not powerful, not wise, and not good, because we cannot make any positive attributions of God. These are all negative attributions. But, for the sake of the religious life, Maimonides believes, we apply to God positive terms, to attribute to God what signifies a perfection in us, power, knowledge, goodness, so as to align ourselves properly with the perfection of God.

Maimonides sees the wisdom of God's actions in the rational structure of reality, including the laws of nature. Indeed, even in his allegedly more popular, legal work, *Mishneh Torah*, Maimonides advises how to achieve love and awe of God. He does not turn to revelation or to God as savior, but to the God of the natural order:

> What is the way to love and fear of [God]? When a person contemplates his great, wondrous creations and creatures and when he sees in them his infinite wisdom, he will at once love, praise, and adulate, and have a great desire to know the great name ... And when he contemplates further on these matters, he will immediately recoil and be fearful knowing that he is a small, lowly and dark, creature with a weak mind before omniscience. (Maimonides, *Mishneh Torah*, Laws of the Foundations of the Torah 2:1–2)

For Maimonides, the love of God is an intellectual love, fueled by an appreciation of God's infinite wisdom, as philosophically and scientifically determined. Fear of God is an initial, undeveloped religious attitude to be replaced in time by awe and wonder at the greatness of God's wisdom, reflected in the world and in philosophical truths. God is behind it all, and so knowing God properly, results in love of God.

Accordingly, in his philosophical writings, Maimonides degrades miracles as much as possible (or entirely, depending on how one interprets his convoluted discussions), a symptom of God's abstract distance from us. And Maimonides equates angels with natural forces (while human-like angelic figures appear as such only in dreams and visions). Love of God does not come from miracles God performs for the Jewish people or for Abraham, Isaac, or Jacob. One who believes because of miracles has "doubt in the heart." And, depending on which Maimonides scholars you believe, he might not have endorsed creation in time at all, instead opting for an Aristotelian always-existing world that eternally depends on God for its existence and orderliness at every moment.

As far as PERSONA-E being a judge, punishing and rewarding, this remains in Maimonides' philosophy, but with a stretched, naturalistic understanding. God punishing people comes to its being the case that people who do not develop a correct understanding of God's world will live willy nilly in our world, dominated as it is by chance events. They will be vulnerable to suffering from chance events. Those who gain a proper understanding of how God's world works (and so are "lovers of God") with their super-knowledge and disciplined character, will understand how to behave so as to avoid as much as possible being given over to mere chance. This will be their "reward" in this life. Seen in this way, the Torah is a collection of laws of reason for an orderly society in which individuals will have the opportunity to flourish by developing their intellectual powers.

In his writings more conventional than the *Guide*, Maimonides is somewhat yielding to more conformist ideas about God. Here is the place to distinguish, as he does, between true and necessary beliefs. (*Guide* 3:28) True beliefs are, well, true. "Necessary beliefs" are not true, or at least not entirely true, but are meant to appeal to the imaginative faculty of non-philosophers. This is in order to arouse in them loyalty to the Torah and are meant to advance civil order. For example, the Torah teaches that God becomes angry. Yet, in truth God has no emotional attributes whatsoever. Yet, it is *necessary* for the Torah to talk that way to put the fear of God in the masses to motivate human behavior for the good.

Maimonides' God is not one meant to be near and responsive, not a God who literally has chosen the Jews as his people, not a God who is at all understandable to his followers. Instead, God is wholly transcendent, a God who can only be thought of by his actions, and that by way of the rational order of the world, a God who does not console you and does not have intimate love for you.

So, what has happened to the God of kindness and mercy, PERSONA-Y? Late in his *Guide for the Perplexed*, 3:53, Maimonides dedicates a chapter to three terms: loving-kindness (*hesed*), justice (*mishpat*), and righteousness/virtuousness (*zedaqah*). See what Maimonides says there about God's loving-kindness:

> In most cases the prophetic books use the word *hesed* [loving-kindness] in the sense of [one] practicing beneficence toward one who has no right at all to claim this from you. Therefore, every benefit that comes from [God], may he be exalted, is called *hesed*. Hence this reality as a whole ... that he has brought into being – is *hesed* ... Accordingly, he is described as hasid (one possessing loving kindness) because He has brought everything into being. (Maimonides, *Guide*, 3:53)

God having loving kindness has nothing to do with the particularism of God choosing the Jews, saving them from Egypt, or bringing them to the Holy Land. God is kind because the entire world and every nation depend on God. Loving kindness is an abstract attribute of God with no specific connection to any nation or person but related equally to the entire cosmos. Since God had and has no obligations to us, everything that happens for the good is thereby an act of loving-kindness.

Thus does Maimonides' God emerge very much with the ruling idea of PERSONA-E, without the threats and the fury. This preference for an abstract, transcendent God met with a caustic rebuttal before Maimonides, by Judah Halevi.

4.3 Judah Halevi

> Look here, friend, use your justice, judgment, think it over, save yourself from mental traps; above all, do not let Greek philosophy seduce you; it may have

flowers, but it never will bear fruit. Or if it does, it only comes to this: the world was not created; and no one stretched the heavens like a tent; and in the beginning there was no creation; the moon will wax and wane forevermore. Just hear the incoherence of their doctrines, constructed out of chaos and pretension; they only leave a hollow in your heart, and nothing in your mouth but syllogisms. Why should I go following such twisting trails, abandoning the mother of all highways?

Judah Halevi (2008, 193–194)

Now, I go back in time from Maimonides (1138–1204), to the philosophy of Judah Halevi (c.1075–1141). Only after having looked at Maimonides can we fully appreciate the subsequent problem of God that weighed on Jewish thought for time after. For what Halevi, poet and philosopher, argues in favor of PERSONA-Y directly applies to Maimonides' philosophy, as well as to Jewish philosophers before Maimonides, prominently to Saadia and Abraham ibn Daud (c. 1110–c.1180).

Judah Halevi (c. 1075–1141) was born in Tudela, Navarre, which today is in modern Spain. He is the most famous Jewish poet of medieval times. His philosophical treatise is named, *The Book of Refutation and Proof in Defense of The Despised Faith.* The book is an imaginary dialogue mainly between a Jewish wise man and the king of the Khazars. The Khazars eventually ruled a large area of Eastern Europe in a time before Halevi, starting around 600 CE. A part of them were reputed to have converted to Judaism, adopting Jewish rituals and Jewish languages, Hebrew and to an extent Yiddish. This was the basis for Halevi's imaginary conversation that convinced the king of the Khazars of the truth of Judaism. The better-known title of the book is thus, *The Kuzari.* Let's call the Jewish wiseman of the book "the rabbi," noting that he speaks for Halevi.

The title gives away the pressures then on Jewish belief from various directions. This included at the time attacks on the Judaism of the rabbis by Christians and Muslims. The attacks also came from a sizable minority of Jews known as the "Karaites," who practiced a Judaism devoid of rabbinic legislation. Halevi is concerned to defeat the Jewish philosophers who to his mind were disfiguring Judaism beyond recognition. Halevi accredited the philosophers when they reasoned correctly but was convinced that fundamentally they had erred.

In *Kuzari,* the rabbi makes an explicit distinction between ELOHIM and YHWH.

The meaning of "ELOHIM" can be grasped by way of speculation, because a guide and manager of the world is a postulate of reason. The meaning of YHWH, however, cannot be grasped by speculation, but only by that intuition and prophetic vision which separates a person so to speak, from his kind, and brings him in contact with angelic beings, imbuing him with a new spirit.

> Then all previous doubts concerning ELOHIM are removed, and [a person] deprecates those speculations by means of which [they] had endeavored to derive the knowledge of God's dominion and unity. It is thus that [a person] becomes a servant, loving the object of worship, and ready to perish for God's sake ... This forms a contrast to the philosophers, who see in the worship of God nothing but extreme refinement ... extolling him in truth above all other beings (4:15).

To this speech the king replies:

> Now I understand the difference between Elohim and YHWH, and I see how far the God of Abraham is different from that of Aristotle. A person yearns for YHWH as a matter of love, taste, and conviction; whilst attachment to Elohim is the result of speculation. A feeling of the former kind invites its votaries to give their life for his sake, and to prefer death to his absence. Speculation, however, makes veneration only a necessity as long as it entails no harm, but bears no pain for its sake.

The God of Halevi is very much our PERSONA-Y, a God of intimate relations, a God who is known by prophecy, intuition, miracles, and revelation. Halevi's God is one to be yearned for and loved, not one who leaves "a hollow in your heart." The God of the philosophers is known, if at all, by human speculation, a far-away God, an abstract reality not engaged within our lives, our foibles, and our successes.

For Halevi, ELOHIM is the God of a philosopher who can put together enough premises to find God as a conclusion. Halevi believed in the God who created and sustained the universe. Not because of speculation, but as God of the Jews, YHWH had revealed that he was the creator. The God of Halevi is the God about whom Pharoah, the non-Jew, once said, "I know not YHWH," (Exodus 5:2) although he does know of ELOHIM.

For Halevi, Jews, and only Jews, have in their souls something divine, translatable variously as a "divine material," "divine thing," or a "divine spark." It is best thought of as an inner divine "stuff" or maybe better as an innate spiritual capacity. Possession of this divine stuff enables prophecy, from an especially sensitive ability to discern God and hear God's voice. Adam had the divine stuff within him, but later on only the Jews had it in them by inheritance.

Accordingly, Halevi's fundamental confession of faith is in the God of history, not the God of the natural order:

> The rabbi replied: I believe in the God of Abraham, Isaac and Israel [Jacob], who led the children of Israel out of Egypt with signs and miracles; who fed them in the desert and gave them the land, after having made them traverse the sea and the Jordan in a miraculous way; who sent Moses with his law, and subsequently thousands of prophets, who confirmed his law by promises to the observant, and threats to the disobedient. (Kuzari 1:11).

For Halevi, the referential chain that fixes the referent of "YHWH," reaches back to the experiences of those to whom God spoke. The referential chain that fixes the referent of "ELOHIM" reaches back to proofs written by the human hand.

In keeping with his preference for PERSONA-Y, Halevi chooses a dynamic reading of the name that God divulges to Moses at the burning bush, in Exodus 3:14: *"eheyeh asher eheyeh."* Grammatically, the name should be read as, "I will be what I will be." Typically, though, translators, including the King James Bible, render it statically as "I am that I am." Philosophers such as Maimonides and Aquinas adopted this static reading as revealing a deep metaphysical truth: that God's existence is identical with God's essence (a long story). Halevi gives the name a dynamic, forward-aiming interpretation instead, as, "I will be present to them whenever they will turn to me," a most appropriate name for PERSONA-Y.

Accordingly, when God self-identifies to the Israelites at the opening of the Ten Commandments in the book of Exodus, says Halevi, the words are "I am the God who took you out of the land of Egypt," not "I am the God who created the world." God is in history, not confined to being beyond the world. This divine self-identification, for Halevi, is the rock-bottom idea of God in Judaism, and stands in direct opposition to Maimonides, who writes in the following way about the foundational belief in God:

> The foundation of all foundations and the pillar of wisdom is to know that there is a first being who brought into being all that exists. All the beings of the heavens, the earth, and what is between them came into existence only from the truth of his being. If one would imagine that he does not exist, no other being could possibly exist. If one would imagine that none aside from him exist, he alone would continue to exist, and their nullification would not nullify his existence, because all the others require him, and he, blessed be he, does not require them nor any one of them. (Mishneh Torah, Foundations of the Torah, Chapter One)

For Maimonides, "the foundation of all foundations" of Judaism is in a philosophical demonstration. For Halevi, "the foundation of all foundations" of Judaism is in historical experiences of God.

Historically, Maimonides' philosophical influence has been largely limited to philosophers and Jewish theologians, and their intellectualist followers. Halevi's thought has had a far wider and lasting impact on the Jewish people than has Maimonides'. The God of Maimonides, an Elohim-God, is too thin, too remote, too cold for most Jews to celebrate as their God. Jews have wanted a God to whom they could turn in times of Jew-hatred, oppression, and massacre, a God of hope and promise. A God who has spoken to them and will speak to them again in future. A God "who will be present to them whenever they will turn" to him. Thus, Maimonides did not make inroads into the Judaism of the masses.

In these two figures, Halevi and Maimonides, we have a profound divide over who the God of the Jews really is. We have seen that Maimonides gives clear preference to outstanding elements of PERSONA-E, while Halevi pulls in the direction of PERSONA-Y. To a significant extend these two medieval philosophers sever the two personae of God one from the other. It will be the Jewish mystical literature that will try mightily to put "Humpty Dumpty" back together again.

5 The Mystical Kabbalah

After Maimonides, there followed an extended period of controversy over his philosophical writings. At one point his writings were burned by a group of Dominicans allegedly at the instigation of anti-Maimonidean Jews (in 1233). Soon after this period of turbulence there appeared major collections of mystical teachings, which proved to have a profound impact on Jewish thought for the ages. This was the "Kabbalah." (For an introduction to Kabbalah see Matt, 2009.)

"Kabbalah" (literally, "what is received") is the name for the Jewish mystical literature, which has its roots in the rabbinic era and in early post-rabbinic Judaism, and quite possibly in Gnostic literature. (See Idel, 1988). Starting in the early second millennium, major Jewish mystical teachings began to appear in the light of day. While there were earlier kabbalistic authors and teachers, a major event was the appearance of *The Book of the Zohar*, (the "Book of Splendor"), in the thirteenth century, to this day virtually the Bible of the kabbalistic tradition. (For an English translation see: Matt, translator, 2018). By tradition, the Zohar was the work of Rabbi Shimon bar Yoḥai, a second-century CE rabbi of the Mishnah, who lived in the Holy Land. According to this tradition the book was secretly passed from generation to generation by a small number of mystical rabbis and was hidden from the masses until its appearance.

There is internal evidence in the Zohar indicating its predominantly later composition than that. (See Scholem, 1995, 163–168, and see Rapoport-Albert and Kwasman, 2006, 5–19.) For example, the book includes Aramaic of a later time than that of the times of the Mishnah, when Rabbi Shimon lived; Spanish and medieval Hebrew terms are sprinkled throughout the book (including some apparent copying from Maimonides) that indicate a later date; and there are several anachronisms as well as gross mistakes about the geography of the Holy Land (where Rabbi Shimon lived).

Today, academic scholars believe that *The Book of the Zohar* was compiled/ written by a small group of kabbalists headed by Moses de Leon (thirteenth century), or by the latter alone. However, devout kabbalists mostly stick to the traditional authorship. One prominent twentieth century kabbalist, Rabbi Yehuda Leib Ashlag (1885–1954), wrote that it really made little difference to him who authored the *Zohar*. Whoever wrote it must have been a Godly person of the first rank, comparable to the image people have of Rabbi Shimon bar Yoḥai.

The second most important source of the kabbalah is the large collection of writings encompassing the teachings of Rabbi Isaac Luria (1534–1572), known as "Ha-Ari" (acronym for the Hebrew "The Godly Rabbi Yitzḥak [Isaac]"). Ha-Ari did not write, rather his students, primarily Rabbi Ḥaim Vital (1542–1620), recorded his teachings. The teachings of Ha-Ari go far beyond the *Zohar* with astounding novelty and intricate detail.

Kabbalah is not a unified teaching, comprising as it does different schools over hundreds of years, with important metaphysical and theological distinctions. Yet, it is possible to write a rough, simplified, outline of the relevant ideas in the *Zohar* and in the kabbalah for our purposes here. Here I will refer to these sources collectively simply as "Kabbalah," but please keep in mind that variants on these occur in the kabbalistic literature. (For an extended study of Kabbalistic symbolism see Wolfson, 1995).

Here I select only one feature from a broad and entangled literature, relevant to us, that pre-occupied the mystical masters. And that is the problem of divine judgment and divine compassion. Here, the kabbalists dedicated themselves to the tireless endeavor of overcoming the powers of *din,* divine judgment, and its dangerous ally, "the other side," the demonic forces of evil. Demonic forces were at the far end of a scale from the attribute of judgment to evil. If Judgment were to become active, the divine forces would be waiting to join in the fun and wreak destruction.

For the kabbalist, the highest form of defense from the threat of Judgment was on behalf of the "divine presence," the *sheḥinah,* in the world. The world-suffering was primarily the suffering of the *sheḥinah* "in exile," cut off by human sins from the supernal worlds and vessels above it. The suffering of the individual kabbalist was an expression of the suffering of the *sheḥinah.* It was the task of the kabbalist to bring the divine presence out of its exile to be included with the rest of the supernal worlds.

This description already says much about the conception of and relationship to PERSONA-ELOHIM in kabbalah. *Din* or Judgment was a constant threat that had to be dealt with forcefully, and this was done by far more than standard Jewish prayer and observance of the laws. The arousing of sufficient divine kindness against those threatening forces, included prominently mystical magic-like practices, with incantations of combinations of Hebrew letters, the infusion of mystical thoughts into the words of prayer, and numerous additions to and amplifications of extant Jewish religious practices.

The aim was to defeat Judgment or at least to mollify it by integrating it with divine compassion, to gain a middle way of "mercy." Here is how it goes. There exists a supernal, supreme reality for the kabbalah, the *Einsof,* the *Infinite,* which lies ineffably beyond any possibility of our knowledge of its essence. (To say it is "infinite" means only that it is not finite.) We can only know of its effects in Reality. (This is similar to Maimonides. But the resemblance stops there.) Reality consists of a descending chain of spiritual worlds emanating from the Infinite One, ending in this our material world. (This is akin, in some ways, to the emanationist doctrine of Plotinus (204/5–270 CE) the neo-Platonic philosopher.).

Because of the ineffability of the Infinite One, we cannot say of it that *it* is kind or strict, loving or punishing, as intrinsic attributes. Rather, all aspects of the Infinite are expressed as attributes of the divine light that emanates from it. The structure of the light in all worlds, those spiritually "above" our world and our material world, is made up of three vertical lines, or channels, of light – right, left, and center. The left side of every structure is the line of justice, judgment, stringency, punishment, and power. The right side is that of love, and kindness. The middle line is (in the main) the result of combining the left and right sides, into *raḥamim*, mercy, that integrates judgment with mercy, grace, holiness, and truth. (There is also so-called "complete mercy," which has no mixture of the left, Judgment, in it.) Sometimes it is said that the middle line "sweetens" the left side (Judgment) by combining it with the right side. (Compassion.) In the words of the work, *Eitz Ḥaim* (*Tree of Life*) by Ḥaim Vital, "The severity of judgment is sweetened within mercy." And the kabbalistic mystic, Menaḥem Azariah da Fano (1548–1620) writes in the name of Isaac Luria that when in prayer one should stand with one's right and left hands over one's heart, with the right hand (indicating Compassion) placed *over* and clutching the left hand (indicating Judgment). This would facilitate the overcoming of the left side, of judgment, by the right side, of kindness. (Azariah da Fano, 1999/2000, Part 2, section 33). This well illustrates how the task of empowering the right over the left side was such an urgent occupation of the Jewish mystics.

Think of the mentioned three lines of light as emanating downward from the Infinite. Along the way, light is captured by "vessels," *ten in number*, that each receives the light for a standing given purpose, revolving around the axes of judgment and compassion. There are two competing interpretations of the status of the vessels. One is that they are divine realities themselves, with powers that they harness from the light emitting from the Infinite, each controlling the light for a different purpose. The other interpretation is functional. The vessels and light are no more than metaphors for functions to which the divine energy is directed. On the left, are the functions aligned with power, justice, judgment, strictness, and law, and on the right functions aligned with beneficence and love. The middle line is aligned with mercy, that enlists the right side to "sweeten," to mollify, the left side, or to neutralize it entirely.

If you go further to the left, from where justice, judgment resides, as it were, you meet the forces of evil looking for ways to break in and work their wickedness, to upset the structure of the divine light either directly or by enticing those below to sin or otherwise disrupt the supernal order. These evil forces are a grotesque distortion and demonic excess of justice, judgment, stringency, and the use of power.

Kabbalah was and is widely accepted by a large band of traditional Judaism as well as by present-day non-traditional Jews drawn to mysticism. Yet, Kabbalah was roundly rejected by some great rabbis over history, who questioned its bona fides. Some also accused kabbalists of believing in a "Tenity" (referring to the ten vessels of the emanations of the Infinite) as anti-monotheistic, to their minds, as was to them the Christian Trinity.

So, we see that the kabbalah envisioned an integration of Judgment and Kindness. Yet, the threat of the left side is constant. For the kabbalah, a fusion of the left side, Judgment, into the middle line and thus to the influence of the right side, compassion, depends to a great extent on the theurgic practices of the kabbalist, practices that dull the dreaded left side and its allied evil forces. The kabbalist executes theurgic techniques to impact the upper spiritual words and the loci ("the vessels") of varied supernal operations, to create a harmonious synthesis of the right side and the left side up there in the spiritual domain. When matters are out of sync in the supernal worlds, say Judgment being dominant there, the same will hold for our world, and when matters are right up there, the light of beneficence will shine down on this world.

The world is a scary place. The responsibilities of the kabbalist included understanding the commandments as ways of influencing the vessels and light to sweeten Judgment, and performing the commandments with that in mind; the meditative manipulation of Hebrew letters in various combinations (without having any meaning in Hebrew); by kabbalistic prayer with *kavanot* (special intent) directing words and letters of the liturgy to the appropriate vessels; giving to the evil spirits a "portion" of what they wanted, hoping they will then go away or be too busy with what they have gotten, to bother the Jews; adding on to Jewish tradition a new array of religious behaviors/actions not known previously, directed to influencing the upper worlds, which in turn will reflect for the good for us here below.

For most of the kabbalists, the Gentile world was included in the forces of evil, at the extreme left of Judgment, and were to be repelled and defeated by the Jews' theurgic practices. Hence, the Jews, and the Jews only, can successfully, theurgically affect the divine light, putting order in the supernal worlds and thus influencing, correspondingly, our world for the good. The responsibilities of the kabbalist were very heavy.

Before condemning this attitude to the Gentile too strongly, one must keep in mind the suffering and agony the Jews were continually enduring from the non-Jewish world, especially from Christians, at the time of the growth of kabbalistic teachers and writings. In the Crusades of the eleventh to thirteenth centuries hundreds of thousands of Jews in the Rhineland, and elsewhere, were slaughtered by the Crusaders on their way to the Holy Land. Jews were murdered, maimed, and plundered by periodic pogroms – local riots often led by the local priest. Jews knew to stay indoors and out of sight of the Christians on special holidays such as Christmas and Easter. Jews were massacred for supposedly being guilty for plagues and for allegedly murdering Christian boys for using the blood in Jewish ritual.

Within a period of a few hundred years in Medieval times, the Jews were expelled from Spain, Portugal, parts of France, Southern Italy, parts of Switzerland, from Hungary, Upper Bavaria, England, Vienna, parts of Russia, and the list goes on. The Jews were also subject to forced conversion to Christianity at various times. Regularly, professions and crafts were forbidden to the Jews. They were prohibited from joining professional guilds, which left them out of pursuing the crafts, such as smithing. Jews were not allowed to own land. And so on. As the world looked to so many Jewish eyes, the Gentile was an evil force that had to be repelled and defeated. Since the Jews could not repel and defeat them with material weapons, they would do so through mystical theurgic practices.

Most indicative of the Jewish mystical literature was the conviction that human practice and intentions would have their effect on the upper worlds of the vessel and the lights, putting our world into proper order by our putting the spiritual worlds above in proper order.

So here is how the kabbalah reflects the central problem of God that occupies us here. For this I will identify God with the *Einsof*, the Infinite, for the latter being the highest instantiation in the supernal realm and the creator of all below it. Kabbalah partly reserves the name "ELOHIM" for the attributes of judgment, punishment, strictness, and power However, the name "YHWH" has a more diverse usage there. "YHWH" can be the name of the Infinite One, but also, the letters "Y-H-W-H" name levels of the vessels on the strings of right, left, and middle. "YHWH" is also the name of one of the vessels in the middle channel of descending light. This identifies YHWH with the integration of judgment with kindness, which in kabbalistic language was called "mercy."

So, first, in kabbalah there is the elevation of the *Einsof* to absolute transcendence, to the point of ineffability. This is a feature suited to PERSONA-E, a god far-away from us conceptually and perceptually. Then there is the pronounced preoccupation with old and new paths to neutralize the power of judgment, by activating the forces of the Y-cluster, or to "sweeten," ELOHIM. A subject that engrosses the kabbalist is how the Jews are to influence, direct, or redirect, by theurgic practices, the supernal forces of divine judgment, and the machinations of diabolic forces. Kabbalah teaches to be steadily occupied with the threat of God's adverse justice, judgment, and the in-a-sense "allied" active powers of evil descending into our world.

As a result, performance of the commandments is no longer simply a matter of doing God's will, but each commandment, done correctly, with proper mystical intent, carries specific theurgic powers. Commandments often aim at and impact specific loci of the divine light – forming intricate combinations of letters and words and manipulating names of God into combinations of letters to influence the higher worlds and the vessels for the good. All of this then reflected down to the world of the kabbalist.

Holy texts hide mystical meanings that must be exposed and theurgically empowered. Likewise, the kabbalist is to decode words of the prayers, to bring to the surface their esoteric meanings, then use them theurgically. And each of the commandments must be "aimed" to influence specific loci of divine vessels and light. A classic example of this is the kabbalistic theurgical understanding of the sounds of the *shofar*, the ram's horn, in the liturgy of the Jewish New Year. The *Zohar* says: "And when the shofar arouses and people repent of their sins, we must sound the shofar here below so that the sound raises above, then a different high shofar is aroused, and it arouses Mercy so that Judgment departs." Each sound of the horn aims at a different supernal vessel that will bring the upper lights of love from above down below and remove the power of Judgment.

For the kabbalist the world is a dangerous place in which to live, where we must be vigilant to keep danger away from us. The kabbalists live under constant threat. So, it is up to them to bring blessing and abundance from above. And they do so by a hefty array of practices, activating salient features of the divine cluster Y to help neutralize E.

In all of this we should stress that as an extension of the rabbinic idea that God needs us as much as we need God, the kabbalah placed great power in our hands here down below to influence the higher spiritual worlds for the better. Our actions could bring the higher worlds into harmonious functioning for the better, in ways that only we could accomplish.

This approach is light years from Maimonides, for whom, as we have seen above, God is a remote reality thin on real mercy. The kabbalists agree with Maimonides that the supreme being is ineffable, but they provide what Maimonides does not, a way to directly engage the *light* of the Infinite One and thus to engage, if only through a medium, *with* the One.

6 Hasidism

When the founder of Hasidic Judaism, the great Rabbi Israel Shem Tov, saw
misfortune threatening the Jews, it was his custom to go into a certain part of
the forest to meditate. There he would light a fire, say a special prayer, and the
miracle would be accomplished and the misfortune averted. Later, when his
disciple, the celebrated Maggid of Mezritch, had occasion for the same reason
to intercede with heaven, he would go to the same place in the forest and say,
"Master of the Universe, listen! I do not know how to light the fire, but I am
still able to say the prayer." Again the miracle would be accomplished.

Still later, Rabbi Moshe-leib of Sasov, in order to save his people once
more, would go into the forest and say, "I do not know how to light the fire.
I do not know the prayer, but I know the place and this must be sufficient." It
was sufficient, and the miracle was accomplished. Then it fell to Rabbi Israel
of Rizhin to overcome misfortune. Sitting in his armchair, his head in his
hands, he spoke to God, "I am unable to light the fire and I do not know the
prayer and I cannot even find the place in the forest. All I can do is to tell the
story, and this must be sufficient."

And it was sufficient.

Martin Buber, *Tales of the Hasidim*

In the eighteenth century, a new movement arose from the kabbalah that
transformed the world for its followers into a much safer place than it is for
the kabbalists. This movement prevails today in a significant sector of traditional Judaism and has influence far beyond that. This is the movement of
Hasidism.

The inspirational figure for the Hasidic movement was the charismatic Israel
Baal Shem Tov (c. 1698–1760), who lived in the Ukraine. In a short number of
years, the movement spread through large parts of Eastern Europe and eventually emerged in all of Eastern Europe and beyond. Today, the main locations of
the Hasidic movement are in Israel and the United States, with small pockets in
Belgium and England, and elsewhere.

Hasidism has as its central interest the transformation of the interior life of the
Hasid (singular for "righteous," plural: "Hasidim"). The metaphysical ten vessels
of the kabbalah become for them more centrally ten psycho-spiritual powers
within the soul of an individual person. A person's interior life then takes place in
the dynamic relations between these powers within her or his soul. This is
a religion with a stark emphasis on inwardness akin to the spirit of inwardness
of Soren Kierkegaard. (For a comparison between Kierkegaard and the Hasidic
Masters, see Gellman, 1994.) And just as Kierkegaard mounted a severe attack on
the Church of Denmark, the early stages of Hasidism included attacks on the
rabbinic establishment of the day. The latter, was the complaint, were not serving

the needs of the Jewish populace, emphasizing learned virtuosity at the expense of inwardness and the simple, religious life of the unlearned.

Fittingly, a motto of Baal-Shem Tov was a verse of Psalm 100, "Worship God with joy; come before him with joyful songs." This motto set the tone for the entire Hasidic movement. Another verse of the Psalms, 2:11: "Serve God with fear, and rejoice with trembling," was less operative than its sister verse. The joy of the religious life, of the encounter of the individual with God, were to be the leitmotif of the Hasidic movement.

Joy was a condition of a fruitful spiritual life. When a person is sad or laden with a sense of self-worthlessness, they will withdraw into themselves, isolating from God and others. They will not progress in their religious life. When happy, a person goes out from themself to be open to the world and to God.

Accordingly, a central religious ethos of Hasidism was a going out of oneself to *devekut*, or "binding," "cleaving" to God in the interior of one's being. As put by the first Hasidic work ever published, by Rabbi Yaakov Yoseph of Polonoya (d. 1782): "for the purpose of the entire Torah is to enable us to bind ourselves to God and love him . . .. The 613 commandments are counsels on how to achieve cleaving to him, may he be blessed" Yaakov (Yoseph of Polonoya 1973/74: volume 1, 7). All of Jewish law has as its telos *devekut*, with the "commandments" becoming "strategies" on how to achieve that purpose. While the Hasidim acknowledged PERSONA-E, their devotion was clearly more to PERSONA-Y, the God of love.

The inspiration for Hasidism, Israel Baal Shem Tov (1698–1760), raised up and propounded that "there is no place devoid of God," which he borrowed from the kabbalistic *Tikunei Zohar*. God is present and palpable for the Hasidim. Much of Hasidism emphasized that the spiritual height of a Jew was to experience her or his self at the core as a Godly soul, a divine light. This core was encrusted over with layers of this-worldly obsessions. Thus, to bind to God was to cut through those crusts and cleave to your true self in your core, your own divine being. Since God was at the core of each of us, each person was able to bind himself to God, and more so, some could do so with little effort.

As one Hasidic Master put it, when at Mt. Sinai God said that "*I* am YHWH *your* God," this meant that the 'I' of a person was a part of God – "your" God, indeed. We have to go beyond our egotistical stance in life to identify with our inner, divine nature. Deuteronomy quotes Moses as saying regarding the revelation at Sinai, "*I* stood between YHWH and you to declare to you the word of YHWH." On this, Baal-Shem Tov said that this means that the "I" the ego, stands between you and YHWH and prevents you from hearing the word of YHWH.

Consequently, some Hasidic masters engaged with God in the most familiar, human terms. An extreme instance of this was the Hasidic master, Rabbi Levi Yitzḥak of Berditchev (1740–1809), who argued with God for the sake of the Jewish people. He charged God with being too strict a father and complained that God should look to the merits of God's people rather than to their sins. It is reported that once the rabbi became so impatient with God's behavior that he spoke these words to God: "Good morning to you, master of the universe. I, Levi Yitzḥak, son of Sarah of Berditchev, I come to you with a court summons from your people Israel" (Dresner, 1974: 86). Levi Yitzḥak complained: "what have you against your people Israel? Why do you pick on your people Israel?"

In the same spirit, Elie Wiesel, the Holocaust survivor who had grown up in a Hasidic milieu, told that while imprisoned in Auschwitz, "I was there when God was put on trial." The story Wiesel tells is this: "I was the only one there. It happened at night; there were just three people. At the end of the trial, they used the word *ḥayav*, rather than 'guilty'. It means 'He owes us something'. Then we went to pray." God was as close to the Hasid as his or her own breath. God was in intimate contact with his creation. The connection was so profound that even when God was found to be at fault, as it were, they then went to pray the evening prayer to God. (see www.thejc .com/news/wiesel-yes-we-really-did-put-god-on-trial-gjs45iw9). I should note, though, that the word *ḥayav* in rabbinic literature can carry the meaning of "guilty."

The God of the Hasidim loved one and all, even the sinners and the unlearned. While often following the precedent of most kabbalah concerning the non-Jews as on the side of evil forces, there were Hasidic masters, such as the above-mentioned Rabbi of Berditchev, who included non-Jews as well in the scope of God's love and mercy.

An untutored person who entered a synagogue with no prior familiarity with the service, might express a yearning for God by suddenly whistling or playing a pocket instrument to God in the middle of the service. God might love that person more than the others who lack in inwardness. Sincerity of heart is what God values above all. We might no longer be able to find the place in the forest, and we might remember neither the prayer nor the way to light the fire, but if we can just tell the story, something inside us will resonate with the divine.

Yes, the Hasid had to deal with divine justice and with the evil powers of the Kabbalah. And this did occupy them. But, unlike in the Kabbalah, in much of Hasidism the Hasid felt ultimately safe because of the forgiving and loving nature of God that so permeated daily experience. Life was much more optimistic for the Hasid than for the other kabbalists.

In particular, God would hide at times from a Hasid, but not for the sake of hiding itself or because of anger. The story is told of a great Hasidic rabbi who when a child ran home crying. His father asked him why he was crying. The boy explained that he had been playing hide-go-seek with friends. He went ahead and hid and then nobody came to look for him. So, he ran home crying. His father then said to him: "Now you know how God feels. God hides and nobody comes to look for Him." God does not hide so as to remain hidden. God plays with us a kind of hide-go-seek. God hides for the joy, on both sides, of being discovered.

For the Hasidic Masters, prayer was the primary way to relate to God, greater than study of the religious texts, which latter was the *sine qua non* of rabbinic teaching. Prayer brought a person into the felt presence of God. And so, Baal Shem Tov, or one of his followers, advised: "When studying [Jewish texts] one must put aside time each hour in order to bind oneself to God." And begrudgingly added, "Even so, one must study." This is a stunning departure from the ethos of the then present rabbinic establishment. For the latter, study of holy texts was the central religious occupation, taking precedence over almost everything else. For Hasidism, purity of heart in relating to God was the center. Intensive study can carry one away from God into the intricacies of the text. The Hasid must take care to bring oneself back to God.

In the Hasidic ethos we see a deepening and broadening of an orientation centrally dedicated to an extension of earlier ideas about PERSONA-Y. The cluster-Y is on the ascendancy in this movement perhaps more than in any other movement in traditional Jewish history. Hasidism stands in stark contrast to Maimonides, whose ethereal philosophical Judaism could hardly take hold in the minds of non-philosophers and the "unwashed masses." Thus, Hasidism included severe criticisms of Maimonides, as by Rabbi Nachman of Breslov (1772–1810), for having replaced genuine faith with an intellectual imposter.

Hasidism thought of faith in God as beyond the reach of philosophical or intellectual reckoning. That does not mean that the Hasid was to have "blind faith," with closed eyes. Far from it. Faith was to come by being open to what could not be formulated fully in conceptual terms, by ascending *l'maalah m'hadaat*, "above cognition," "above reasoning," to a realm beyond. A common analogy to this among the Hasidim is to a young child who first begins to call her mother, "Mommy." We who observe this impose a conceptual meaning on this term: a "mommy" is a mother, one who gave birth to the child or who has adopted the child as her own. But for the little girl, the word "Mommy" has no conceptual content. Instead, it is a direct reference to the person the child has come to recognize and appreciate on multiple occasions. It is a kind of pointing to that very person. Just so, the Hasid is asked to be open to recognizing God's very presence on multiple occasions, to know God by direct reference, unencumbered by intellectual baggage. This is a celebration of PERSONA-Y. The Hasidic ethos may be reflected most radically in this Hasidic comment on the Confession for Sins said on Yom Kippur, the yearly Day of Atonement. The following is attributed to Rabbi Yitzhak Meir Alter (1799–1886) one of the giants of the movement and founder of the Gur group of Hasidism. In this text the Rabbi uses "Depart from evil and do good" from Psalms 34:14, in a novel way, to mean: depart from, get away from, thinking about your sins. Don't wallow in the sins you have committed. Instead, "Do good."

When a person focuses on "Depart from evil" (Psalms 34:14) they are thinking of mud. No matter how much you turn mud over it remains mud. You did sin! You didn't sin! What does the Blessed Holy One get from all of that?! While thinking of the sins you could instead be declaring pearls and then there would be something for the Kingdom of Heaven in it. Therefore, do *depart* from the evil, that is, turn yourself away from *thinking* of the evil [you have done], don't think about the evil. Instead, if you did a pack of sins now do a pack of good deeds, "Do Good!" (Psalms 34:14) You must calmly feel the abandonment of sin. Accept it in your heart and then rejoice. On Yom Kippur then say the confessions of sin (*al het*) quickly, don't wallow in it.

> When a person focuses on "Depart from evil" (Psalms 34:14) they are thinking of mud. No matter how much you turn mud over it remains mud. You did sin! You didn't sin! What does the Blessed Holy One get from all of that?! While thinking of the sins you could instead be declaring pearls and then there would be something for the Kingdom of Heaven in it. Therefore, do *depart* from the evil, that is, turn yourself away from *thinking* of the evil [you have done], don't think about the evil. Instead, if you did a pack of sins now do a pack of good deeds, "Do Good!" (Psalms 34:14) You must calmly feel the abandonment of sin. Accept it in your heart and then rejoice. On Yom Kippur then say the confessions of sin (*al het*) quickly, don't wallow in it.

7 Modern Jewish Philosophy

Meanwhile, back in philosophy. Here, there follow three modern Jewish philosophers who self-identified as engaging with the tradition, and whose thought was especially significant in the history of dealing with the two divine personae: Hermann Cohen (1842–1918) Franz Rosenzweig (1886–1929), and Abraham Joshua Heschel (1907–1972). Herman Cohen, of the Jewish Reform movement, tries to find a way to retain and raise up salient characteristics of both PERSONA-E and PERSONA-Y. Rosenzweig and Heschel (a neo-Hasid) represent each a lurch into the arms of the God of love and mercy.

7.1 Herman Cohen (Joseph Yossi Turner)

Herman Cohen (1842–1918) was a most important Jewish philosopher, from the last decade of the nineteenth century until the end of World War I. He is considered by some to be the Maimonides of Jewish modernity. Just as no one compares to Maimonides, in the navigation of the meeting of Judaism and Greek philosophy in the middle-ages, so, it is thought, no post-emancipationist thinker navigated the stormy sea of engagement between the traditional Jewish heritage and modern philosophical discourse as thoroughly and as skillfully as did Herman Cohen.

Cohen grew up in a family that bore a strong affiliation with classical Reform Judaism, though it retained features of the old tradition. Reform Judaism grew out of the civil emancipation of the Jews in European Society. Generally, Reform Judaism sees Jewish law as rather otiose, following upon the social and cultural integration of the Jews into modern societies. Theologically, it identifies the ethical messianism of Israel's prophets with the ideal ethical vision of modern humanism.

After becoming quite familiar with the Jewish literary heritage already as a child, through intensive textual study with his father, Cohen expanded his study of Jewish texts as a student at the Jewish Theological Seminary, in Braslau, headed by Zecharia Frankl (1801–1875). Following his studies at the Seminary, he studied philosophy at a number of German universities, following which he joined the faculty at the University of Marburg. There he founded what came to be known as the Marburg School of Neo-Kantianism, while gaining a reputation as one of Germany's most important philosophers.

When he reached the age of retirement, Cohen moved to Berlin and taught philosophy in the Jewish Reform seminary (Hochschule für die Wissenschaft des Judentums). During this time, he wrote his most famous book: *The Religion of Reason from out of the Sources of Judaism.*

What arises from Cohen's book is a conception of divinity that does not quite choose between the clusters of divine attributes, Y and E, but maintains salient features of each. Medieval philosophy presumed that by extending the chains of its own logic from the immanent to the transcendent it had direct access to the metaphysical horizon from which the divine attributes were derived. For the modern neo-Kantian Cohen, however, there can be no knowledge of any form of reality, without the human spirit being already involved in the construction of that reality in experience. (See Poma, 1997: 55ff.)

In his earlier writing, Cohen related to God as an immanent idea created by universal reason, and to religion as a sub-category of ethics. But in his later writing, he follows Maimonides in referring to God not only as an idea, but also as Transcendent Being. (See Poma, 1997, 232.) God is more than distant; He is the absolute Other from whom flows both the rational order of creation and the ethical ideal of universal justice. So far, this fits PERSONA-E.

But, with the same power and with logical consistency, Cohen also takes the attributes previously associated with PERSONA-Y very seriously. Though God, for him, is primarily a universal God of truth and justice, it is vital, for his system, that He also be a personal God who can be prayed to, a saving God who is perceived as providential.

The point is that while Cohen primarily sees divinity in rational, universal, and ethical terms, as does Maimonides, his logic is different. At best, the divine attributes can be perceived as a product of the relation between divine Transcendence and the human spirit that precedes their formulation, but not of Transcendence, in and of itself. This does not mean, for Cohen, that there is nothing intrinsic to God that justifies our speaking of certain attributes as divine, or that justifies our speaking of him as creator. The fact that there is a logical relation between the existence of the empirical world and the Transcendent mystery of being, is a given, but how that given relation is perceived comes from the human side of the divine–human correlation. (Poma, 1997, 187–234.)

Since the divine attributes are not of God alone, but of the reciprocal relation between divine Transcendence and the human spirit, the concrete qualities of justice and mercy, promises of salvation, etc., can never be descriptive of God as such. A proper understanding of Herman Cohen's perception of God requires that we understand that all attributes ascribed to God are jointly created by the actual presence of divine Transcendence on the metaphysical horizon of human subjectivity, on the one hand, and the human spirit as it responds to its pre-perceived relation with the Transcendent, on the other.

Divine Attributes: Expression of Divine Being or Human Ascription

For Cohen, as for Maimonides, the literary source of the divine attributes, is Exodus 34, where God responds to the request just made by Moses, to know Him, by declaring Himself to be manifest in His being "merciful and gracious, long-suffering, abundant in love and Truth, keeping love unto the thousandth generation, forgiving iniquity, transgression, and sin," etc. Distancing himself from more traditional interpretations of scripture that emphasize in these verses only the attributes of mercy, Cohen affirms the image of the vengeful God at the end, who punishes the children for the iniquity of the parents even after a few generations. He also follows Maimonides in saying that statements concerning the divine attributes do not reflect divine Being in and of itself – for "no human can see Me and live," but are rather "conceptually determined models for the action of man." (Cohen, 1972, 95.)

But there is also a deep difference between Cohen and Maimonides. For Maimonides, the attributes of action presume the logic of divine reason already active in creation, but because of the limits of human cognition, human beings cannot know how they follow from the divine. Cohen, because of his modern humanist bent, presumes an ontological divine–human correlation that precedes the formation of the attributes ascribed to divinity. (Poma, 1997, 230–232.)

The Meaning of God in the Divine–Human Correlation: Being, Becoming and Purpose

To understand Cohen properly, it is important to note why biblical Monotheism is superior, for him, to Pagan mythology. Mythology represents a primitive form of causality in which even divinity is described as an already present Being. In Monotheism, on the other hand, "the place of causality is taken by purpose" as it "elevates [the divine] characteristics to norms."

By rooting the idea of humanity (along with all facets of existence) in the appearance of God, at one pole of the divine–human correlation, Cohen provides an ontological basis for ethics that is missing in much modern humanist philosophy. He adds the fundamental intuition that the ethical obligations of humanity are not a result of the ethical construction of the human spirit alone, but that the human spirit, particularly that which created ethical Monotheism, constructed its ideal of humanity following a sense of being commanded by one's creator. The command is common to religion and ethics. The divine–human reciprocity, from which religion follows, simply adds, in this context, the religious experience of standing and being commanded "before God" to the parameters of ethical obligation known to philosophical discourse.

From a purely logical perspective, being and becoming are reciprocal. Without "being" there could be no "becoming," but without "becoming" "being" would be a senseless concept. Similarly, for Cohen, without the absolute Being of divine Transcendence there could be no existence in the "becoming" of nature and humanity. But by the same token, transcendent Being could never be perceived as a creating, revealing and commanding God, had it not been for the historical "becoming" of human existence and of the human spirit to the point that it conceives of Him as such.

Holiness, Repentance, and the Messianic Age

It is no coincidence that the "purposive" character of the divine attributes, in the Religion of Reason, echoes the practical content of ethics in modern philosophy. Making social and moral values as justice, ethical responsibility, and compassion for one's neighbor the measuring rod for one's humanity, is common to biblical prophecy and modern humanism. The ideal of ethics, posited by reason, and the ideal humanity envisioned by the prophets, ultimately constitute, for Cohen, the same ideal, and are tied to the same ethical responsibility.

From here follows Cohen's unique understanding of "holiness," (see Poma, 1997, 192–198) in ethical Monotheism. The command to be holy is essentially a command to realize the ideal ethical norms embodied in the divine attributes of action. But note the reciprocal character "Thou shalt be Holy – *for* I am Holy, the eternal, your God." This is a call from Being to becoming. God is Holy, because the human side of the divine–human correlation ascribes to divine Transcendence, a "holy spirit" constituted by the ideals of justice and mercy. Holiness for the human, on the other hand, is the spiritual response to the command arising from the attribute to do mercy and justice. Holiness for God and Holiness for the human, he says, must be two different things. "God has to remain God and man – man." And yet, "holiness unifies God and man," insofar as it "unambiguously defines itself as human morality" and is achieved through a process of "self-sanctification."

Repentance, for Cohen, is the process of self-sanctification, made in response to the command to be holy, (Cohen, 1972, 60–61, 192–195, 198, 201–206) and thus reflects the divine–human correlation. In consequence with the principles of his neo-Kantian ethics, Cohen thought that it is absolutely necessary that the human being be considered worthy of divine atonement, only on the basis of an autonomous act of ethical transformation. He seemed to further believe that human progress toward an ideal humanity as mandated by philosophical ethics was not possible without repentance, and that repentance was not possible without it occurring "before God."

Cohen's understanding of what it means to be standing before God is taken from the following statement, attributed to the second century sage, Rabbi Akiva: " . . . O Israel, Who purifies you?" and "before whom are you purified? – It is [before] your Father in Heaven." Cohen took this statement to express the divine–human correlation with respect to the concepts of repentance and atonement. "Before whom are you purified?" The ethical commands both obligates and enables repentance, but repentance as purification can only be an act of self-transformation. "Before whom are you purified?" For Cohen, the ethical self-sanctification of the human being, can only succeed if it is done in the existential context of standing "before God."

Here, for Cohen, is the significance of God as both an abstract universal God of justice, highlighting aspects of PERSONA-E and a concrete merciful God who listens to prayer and saves the unfortunate from suffering, closer to PERSONA-Y. Because the presence of divine Transcendence on the horizon of human understanding was translated, in the national spirit of ancient Israel, into the idea of God as creator of the universe, the image of the creator God is necessarily associated, in biblical monotheism, with all aspects of the created world, including the anger and seeming punishment characteristic of human existence because of poverty, violence, sickness, and the like; as well as manifest through blessings of grace. The point is that for Cohen, the Religion of Reason organizes all aspects of divine creation as following from the metaphysical pole of divine–human reciprocity, ascribing them with ethical purposiveness, while the response given on the human side of this reciprocity is reflected in the religious act of repentance.

God is central to Cohen's concept of repentance because of the way in which the Religion of Reason conflates the divine image with the ethical ideal, while directing the self's attention to the fate of the "fellow-man" and to the obligation of bearing responsibility for him. (Cohen, 1972, 143, 189, 193, 201–204.) The prophets of Israel, according to Cohen, liberated the religious demand for atonement from its mythical moorings. They did this by imagining God as One whose threat of punishment projects ethical transgression as a blight on creation, and views self-transformation as essential for the ethical completion of creation through the realization of the divine ideal in the future. (Cohen, 1972, 178–215). This is truly the image of God as a God of justice and of judgment, close to salient features of PERSONA-E. But God is also central to repentance because He is, at one and the same time, a God of mercy and compassion, PERSONA-Y. The author of all creation promises that a serious attempt to return to one's ideal divine nature will be met with success.

Thus, in Cohen's mind, "repentance is self-sanctification" in the sense intended by the prophet Ezekial who spoke of the command to repent as the command to create for one's self, and perhaps for all of humanity, "a new heart and a new spirit." (Cohen, 1972, 203). The divine side of the divine–human correlation arouses the ideal, while the human works to realize that ideal through the actualization of the divine image within.

The messianic vision of the prophets is conceived, in this context, as a projection by the Religion of Reason, on the fundamental divine–human correlation, insofar as the prophetic vision seems to stand by divine promise. But this ultimately depends on the ethical success of human endeavor. The prophets, for Cohen, envisioned a time when all of humanity will have achieved a state of ethical holiness as a result of the universal acceptance of the Religion of Reason and its demand for ethical self-transformation. Put differently, it is the vision of a time in which all of humanity will live "before God." (Poma, 1997, 235–262.)

7.2 Franz Rosenzweig (Joseph Yossi Turner)

Franz Rosenzweig (1886–1929) was one of the most important twentieth century religious thinkers. Rosenzweig sought to re-establish divine revelation as the focus of religious discourse following earlier humanist tendencies. For him, Judaism has an important role to play in the redemption of humanity, because the Jewish people anticipate the ultimate redemption, and thereby represent to the world the goal they must ever pursue. The implications of his thought for the problem of conflicting attributes ascribed to God owes to his unique position regarding the inter-relationship of creation and revelation in human experience.

The Legitimacy of Anthropomorphism

Rosenzweig adopted from Herman Cohen, a vision of divine–human reciprocity. But rather than understand this in terms of a logical co-relation, he joined Martin Buber in conceiving the divine–human correlation in existential terms, as a concrete dialogue between the finite human self and God as eternal Thou. (See Bergman, 1991, 206–208.) Cohen therefore justified the Biblical descriptions of God in concrete, corporeal and even human form, because the attributes ascribed to the divine "are throughout assertions about meetings between God and man." "God hears, speaks, gets angry and loves" because "theological experiences, so long as they are genuine ... are experiences of meetings." (Rosenzweig, 1998, 138).

Revelation in the Understanding of God, Man, and World

Rosenzweig's most famous book is entitled *The Star of Redemption*. (Rosenzweig, 1998) Redemption, in this book, refers to both an existential redemption, through revelation, of the individual human being from his initial state of tragic existence as a mortal creature, as well as to the end of days in which all of existence will be redeemed from its tragic fate by the very same light of revelation. In this chapter we shall speak primarily of revelation in the first sense.

Existence Before the Abyss of Nothingness

Following Nietzsche, Rosenzweig presumed that all culture, science and philosophy are the result of an attempt to escape the tragic quality of human existence and its confrontation with mortality. The *Star* therefore begins with the words: "From death, from the fear of death begins all cognition of the All." "All that is mortal," Rosenzweig says, inevitably "lives in the fear of death" insofar as "every new birth multiplies the fear for it multiplies that which is mortal." In response to the fundamentally tragic experience of human mortality, he says, "philosophy smiles its empty smile and with its outstretched finger shows ... [to] the creature whose limbs are trembling ... a world beyond that he did not request ... ." Philosophy, he thought, ought to begin with the concrete human being who "does not want to escape," but rather "wants to live."

Paradoxically, he speaks of mortality as both the "keystone" of creation and the "headstone" of revelation. This is because confrontation with one's mortality requires a willingness to stand at the edge of one's momentary existence while staring into the surrounding abyss. To speak of death as the "keystone" of creation is to speak of human experience when all worldly existence is thrown back behind the present moment and all that is left is the "end" of life itself. Rosenzweig considered this a necessary condition for the realization of a direct encounter with divine presence and therefore saw the confrontation with mortality to be the "foundation stone" of revelation. Once a person ceases to flee and looks into the abyss, there occurs the possibility of hearing a divine voice and of witnessing the revelation of divine presence from within that abyss.

On this backdrop, the harsh and impersonal attributes of anger and judgment, included in PERSONA-E, and the close, personal attributes of love and mercy, of PERSONA-Y, reflect, respectively, the indirect human encounter with divinity in the world of creation, and a direct encounter with the divine in revelation.

Existence: Between Creation and Revelation

The act of creation, of course, precedes human experience and has its origin in the realm of divine Transcendence. Creation is an act of divine grace since it is the beginning of life, and therefore already contains a potential for the renewed revelation of divine grace to the mortal self. But the experience of the "good" described as divine grace cannot dominate human life in the day-to-day existence of the created world, because of its objectivity. In the philosophical language he shares with Martin Buber, the created world is experienced as an I–it relation, and not as an I–You relation as found in a direct encounter with another. Therefore, in the created world, Rosenzweig maintains, the human creature can only experience himself as a lifeless or objective phenomenon, against which the will to live rebels. (See Turner, 2014a)

In revelation, on the other hand, the human being finds himself in a direct and concrete dialogical relation with divinity, and therefore experiences life in an ultimate sense. Here the human self is temporarily freed from the psychological effects of mortality while experiencing a supreme sense of fulfillment in the depths of his being.

Revelation as a Dialogue of Love and Grace

To elucidate his idea of revelation and its implications, Rosenzweig turns to the great Jewish sage from the second century, Rabbi Akiva, who fought for the inclusion of *The Song of Songs* in the biblical canon; and even designated it as "the Holy of Holies," in contrast to the other books of the Bible which he described simply as "Holy." According to Rosenzweig, Rabbi Akiva understood the Jewish Torah and its commandments as the canonical expression of God's encounter with the human in a revelation of love, with the additional clarification that when speaking of love, what is divine is also human and what is human is also divine. Referring to such verses as: "I am for my Beloved as my Beloved is for me"; "Your cheeks are beautiful with earrings, your neck with strings of jewels"; and "Behold, thou art fair, my love; fair; thine eyes are as doves," Rosenzweig says: "Man loves because God loves and as God loves" (Rosenzweig, 1998, 199, 213–214.).

Rosenzweig was not a religious fundamentalist who believed that the Torah was miraculously handed to the children of Israel at Mt. Sinai. But he did believe that the Torah is the word of God as spoken through the word of man. For him, the same word God spoke in creation when he said: "Let there be Light!," is present in the commandment in Leviticus, to love God and to love one's neighbor; as if to say, God's command to be, in creation, is ultimately realized in the human capacity to love and be loved in the context of revelation. The divine word of creation is directed at the world but when heard by the individual soul, in revelation, it becomes a call to which one cannot but respond.

In this manner he understands the call: "Where art thou?," with which God turns to Adam following the eating of the forbidden fruit in the Garden of Eden. Adam does not respond as a concrete mortal subject but rather places the blame for his transgression on others. The proper response is first given by Abraham in the story of the binding of Isaac, where he answers by saying: *Hineni* (Here I am). "Where art thou?" This is none other than the quest for the Thou ... To God's "Where art thou?" the man had ... kept silent ... Now, called by his name ... he answers ... all ready, all soul: "Here I am." (Rosenzweig, 1998, 175–177, 189–192.)

God's call to Adam and to Abraham reflects the dialogical character of revelation, as an I–You relation, in opposition to the narrational I–it character of the world as given in creation.

The main difference between a theology of revelation, which presumes the centrality of encounter with the divine, and one which presumes a predetermined conception of divinity, is that the former considers divinity only through its act of self-transcendence in which it becomes immediately present to the human. Revelation is the epitome of all I–You relations. It is a relation in which two subjects become present to each other – as subjects. Therefore, not only does divinity, which remains for the human being an utter mystery, transcend itself to become present to the human in revelation, but in response the human also transcends himself and becomes present to God.

For Rosenzweig, ultimately there is only one commandment, for which all the rest are mere commentary. This is the command to Love as an existential repercussion of the love relation itself.

The summons to hear . . . the seal of the divine speaking mouth, all these are but preface to . . . that one commandment . . . which in truth . . . . is the only commandment, the sum and substance of all the commandments to leave God's mouth . . . 'Thou Shalt love the Lord thy God, with all thy heart, with all thy soul and with all thy might'. op.cit.

That love can only be commanded by the lover refers to the experience of love in which the love of the lover, of God, arouses the love of the beloved in the human to a point that "overflows the banks" of one's soul, thereby erasing, if only temporarily, the paralyzing fear of death.

But then he asks, what does it mean to say that one is commanded to love God? Can love be commanded?" This is indeed a paradox: "Love cannot be commanded" unless it "proceeds from the mouth of the Lover. . . . Only the lover can and does say: Love me. . . . In his mouth . . . it is none other than the voice of love itself."

For Rosenzweig, even though the divine commandment may be perceived by the human subject in the already created world, it is already an aspect of revelation. Creation and revelation are, for him, but different experiences and vantage points in the same reality. The creation of the world was an act of grace in that it was the beginning of life. Revelation is the very same act, when pointed directly at the suffering human soul. Grace is experienced as love and the experience of love reveals the divine presence that already informs creation.

This is why Rosenzweig follows Rabbi Akiva in viewing the The Song of Songs as the ultimate literary expression of revelation. We already saw, for him, that the human loves only "because God loves and as God loves." The human love depicted in the Song of Songs is therefore necessarily already divine love.

Rosenzweig finds support for his position regarding the role of revelation with respect to the tragedy of human existence in the one verse of The Song of Songs, that stands in sharp contrast to the dialogical character of love expressed throughout. This is the verse that states that "love is as strong as death." "In the whole of the book," he writes, "there is only one brief passage where the I remains silent . . . This passage stands out prodigiously just as we are aware of the ticking of a clock only when it suddenly stops. These are the words of love which is as strong as death. . . . Death is the ultimate point and the fulfilled end of Creation – and love is as strong as it is" (Rosenzweig, 1998, 201–202, 217).

Conclusion: Love and the Redemption of Humanity

How does this conception of revelation add to our discussion of the divine attributes? We saw that revelation, for Rosenzweig, redeems the human soul from the tragic effects of mortality. This is the work of our PERSONA-Y. But after every love experience there is a return to the mundane world, and the soul once again finds itself in a realm ruled by the anonymous forces of law and retribution, at the end of which comes the subjects own demise. Here one encounters PERSONA-E. Because of the infinite distance between the momentary existence of the mortal human being and the perceived eternity of the divine, God's love can never be totally contained within the fleeting experience of the individual in revelation. There is always a residue that is carried into the future with the hope and expectation for a "renewal of the miracle" (See Turner, 2014b, 173–193). The divine presence has passed on to other moments, distant from the individual's concern with his own fate. And yet, the potential for a renewal of the revelatory experience is now present and conscious. The human will to live, in creation, is now able to join the epistemic turn of the beloved in "hope and expectation" for the renewal of revelation, in a way that commands the human subject to extend the divine love, already experienced, forward, as love of the neighbor.

Rosenzweig thus understands the divine commandment: "Thou shalt Love Your neighbor as yourself" to be a direct continuation of the command to Love God. Both are made possible by the same divine Grace, and in the end, for Rosenzweig, human love is the very same divine love that the beloved experienced in divine revelation, but which now extends through human activity to another. It is as though human love is both an after-shock of the initial experience of direct divine revelation, and a human act that initiates a trans-historical process meant to bring about the ultimate redemption of humanity, which he refers to as "the Coming of the Kingdom."

All these are aspects of the relation that Rosenzweig anthropomorphically describes as an encounter of love and mercy between God and man. Judgment and suffering are ever present in so far as the created world in which we live our day to day lives is incomplete and we are constantly forced to relive the fact of our mortality. Nonetheless his understanding of divine love as the root of all existence is also always ever-present and gives hope for the future. Rosenzweig, above all, celebrates the God of PERSONA-Y.

7.3 Abraham Joshua Heschel

The great researcher of Jewish mysticism, Gershom Scholem, once wrote that Hasidism was a harbinger of modernity. This is true in two ways. One is the emphasis on the internal life of the individual devotee (but without losing sight of the community). This is similar to the turn of the Danish philosopher Soren Kierkegaard to "inwardness" during the time that Hasidism was flourishing in Eastern Europe. The second is in its pronounced turn to the God of mercy and tending away from the God of judgment. (I emphasize here that this is true only overall, with notable exceptions along the way.) This was to set a direction in Jewish thought in which the God of dire judgment is marginalized or appropriately reconstrued. The Neo-Hasidic movement, marked by thinkers indebted to Hasidic thought, carried on with this departure from a firm duality in God. The leading thinker of this group is Abraham Joshua Heschel.

In the twentieth century, the Hasidic mood of engagement with God within the Jewish tradition was developed most famously by Rabbi Abraham Joshua Heschel (1907–1972).

Heschel came from an illustrious Hasidic family, with Hassidic rabbis on both his mother's and his father's side. His namesake was the Hasidic rebbe Abraham Joshua Heschel (1748–1825), who was rabbi in Apt (Opatow), Poland, a member of the all-time All-Star team of Hasidism. Our Heschel expanded on Hasidic thinking bringing it up to date in the world of the second half of the twentieth century. Many books commemorate his genius and numerous contributions to both Jewish and non-Jewish religious life. He made major contributions to biblical, rabbinic, Medieval, and Hasidic thought, and was a major shaper of contemporary Jewish thought. Here, I concentrate on Heschel's contribution to the ongoing problem of God in Judaism. We find in his writings a decided turn to the God of compassion and love. This is complicated by Heschel's saying that God is ineffable, as in his *Man is not Alone* (1951). But that must be left for another time.

Heschel may be called "neo-Hasidic" for several reasons. He restated and updated old Hasidic teachings into a contemporary form. He widened the vision of traditional Hasidism beyond addressing only Jews and its having applied Hasidic teachings only to Jews. He engaged deeply in inter-religious conversation and action, hardly a core Hasidic value. In a lecture entitled, "No Religion is an Island," at the Union Theological Seminary in New York, in 1966, he said: "The religions of the world are no more self-sufficient, no more independent, no more isolated than individuals or nations. Energies, experiences and ideas that come to life outside the boundaries of a particular religion or all religions continue to challenge and to affect every religion (Heschel, 1966: 6).

To Heschel, the basic truth was that God was in search of "man." As he then put it: "All of human history as described in the Bible may be summarized in one phrase: *God is in search of man.* ... When Adam and Eve hid from his presence, the Lord called: *Where* art thou (Genesis 3:9). It is a call that goes out again and again (Heschel 1955: 13).

And what does God look for in us: "[The Bible's] concern is with man and his relation to the will of God. The Bible is *the quest for the righteous man*, for a righteous people."

Heschel then quotes the following from (Psalms 14:2–3) for his proof text: "The Lord looks down from heaven upon the children of man, to see if there are any that act wisely, that seek after God. They have all gone astray they are all alike corrupt; there is none that does good, no, not one."

God seeks us to partner with the divine desire to bring justice to those who suffer or are in want: "God and man have a task in common as well as a common and mutual responsibility" (Heschel 1955, 286.). So, God's concern for humanity is that we cooperate to promote God's desire for justice to be done in the world. So, what God wants from humanity God also wants for God as well. In Heschel, we find a strong identification with a God who has ultimate concern for humanity, with concern that we do justice for the poor and unfortunate, for the repressed and abused. This is a God for whom the demand *for us to do justice* is mostly what makes God a "God of justice." This motif echoes that strand of rabbinic teaching, that we have seen, in which God is in need of us, that has God saying, "We need each other."

Heschel did not only talk the talk. He also, literally, walked the walk. He became an icon of Jewish support for civil rights for the Blacks in America, when in 1965 he walked together with Martin Luther King, in Selma, Alabama, for the civil rights of Blacks in the United States. Later he said that in Selma, "my feet were praying." He also worked for religious understanding between Judaism and other religions, most famously in his engagement with the historic Catholic Church's *Nostra Aetate* declaration on Jews, of 1965. (See Furnal, 2016)

***

Heschel brought the Hasidic ideal of "simple faith" to a contemporary formulation by advocating against an intellectual approach to God and in favor of a person opening her or his self to what was above intellectual formulation. The way to God, then, was wonder, wonder at the world, at revelation, and at the human soul, opening one's being to God. "Wonder or radical amazement is the chief characteristic of the religious man's attitude toward history and nature" (Heschel, 1959, 45).

A major contribution of Heschel to our study was his extensive defense of divine *anthropopathy*, that God has emotions and desires, concerns and anguish. Rejecting anthropomorphism, that God has a body, Heschel roundly endorsed the prophetic experience of God's deeply felt emotions. Paramount was God's concern for "Man," so that one of Heschel's most famous books is entitled, *God in Search of Man*. God cares for humans and seeks them out with love and with a demand that justice be pursued on earth.

Heschel notes that in Greek thought God has no emotions, because emotions for the Greeks "belonged to the animal nature in man, reason to the divine" (Heschel, 1955, 250). In addition, for God to respond emotionally would make God be affected by others, whereas God was perfect, self-determining, and self-sufficient in all matters. This line was followed in the main by some in Medieval Jewish philosophy as well, having accepted the Stoic view that "All passion is evil," with emotions being a disturbance to the intellect. Accordingly, God was to have no passions, and persons too were to strive for *apatheia*, apathetic non-disturbance by emotions, to be like God in achieving complete freedom from emotions. (Heschel, 1955:253).

For Heschel, on the contrary, "None of the passions are in themselves bad: they are simply natural, but in order to become ethical they require training." For the Hebrew prophets, says Heschel, God's emotions are not wild and untamed, an interference with sound thinking and proper aims. God's emotions are moral in nature, from love and concern for human beings. God's emotions have clear moral aims and are well formed and constructive, a matter of decision and determination.

God may have no body but has emotions and desires of the highest order. To be sure, anthropomorphism is to be rejected. But anthropopathy, divine pathos, is absolute selflessness with supreme concern for others. So, divine pathos is not to be compared to human emotions, and for Heschel this means that, unlike anthropomorphism, anthropopathy is a perfection of God and not a lowering of God's stature.

Well, what about the judging God? The punishing God? Does he have no place in Heschel's scheme of things? The answer is that for Heschel, God is a God of justice primarily as one who cares infinitely about people doing justice in human affairs. God cares that justice be done on earth for the weak, for the disempowered, for the abused, for the widows and orphans – and for the Blacks, such as on those momentous days in Selma, Alabama. This is very different from the classic picture of the Old Testament God who is "just" because of visiting exact punishment upon those who defy his Word as well as affording justice to those who follow in his ways.

Let's look closely at what Heschel says about God and justice. In a chapter of his entitled "Justice," (Heschel, 1955, 195–220). Heschel, as do the Hasidim, methodically downplays God's dispensing exact justice. The key for him is that "God is a righteous judge." Heschel quotes Isaiah 30:18

Therefore, God is waiting to be gracious to you;
Therefore, He exalts Himself to show mercy to you.
For God is a God of justice.
Blessed are those who wait for Him.

God is righteous in justice.

And Heschel writes: "Righteousness goes beyond justice. Justice is strict and exact, giving each person his due. Righteousness implies *benevolence, kindness, generosity ... Righteousness is* associated with a burning compassion for the oppressed" (Heschel, 1955, 201)

Therefore, "It would be wrong to assume that there was a dichotomy of *mishpat* [judgment] and kindness" (Heschel, 1955, 201)

So here is the punchline. God's justice is ruled by God's concern and totally absorbed into God's compassion: "Divine Justice involves God being merciful, compassionate" (!) (Heschel, 1955, 201). God is "the God of justice," because of God's desire that justice be done, that *we* be just. Heschel pretty much downplays a straightforward understanding of God's *punishing* us for our sins, in favor of God's passion for *our doing justice*, a passion driven by compassion for the unfortunates. Heschel translates "God's concern for justice, as growing out of His concern for man" (Heschel, 1955, 216). In this way an original element of the E-cluster, God as judge, becomes replanted and transformed into the Y-cluster.

Well, what about the many passages of the Torah and Prophets that depict God's anger and wrath? Are these not indicative of a vindictive God? For Heschel, the answer is that God's anger is roused because of *our* doing insufferable injustice, and so is only a result of God's kindness and compassion. For Heschel, God's anger is "righteous indignation," an "impatience with evil" and "the soul rousing itself to curb sins" (Heschel, 1955, 283). "The prophets never thought that God's anger is something that cannot be accounted for, unpredictable, irrational. It is never a spontaneous outburst, but a reaction occasioned by the conduct of man" (Heschel, 1955, 282).

Never, Heschel writes, are mercy and graciousness separable from the thought of God in the Bible (Heschel, 1955, 290). Finally, anger is not an essential attribute of God, for Heschel, as testified by God rarely described as an "angry God," as opposed to a "merciful" or "righteous" God. Anger is an activity of God's compassion, not a divine attribute. Indeed, Heschel also has little use for the word "sin."

Now this kind of God can be made out only by ignoring cases of God's anger that do not fit Heschel's divine configuration of compassion. For example, when in 2 Samuel, 6:6–8, David is bringing the ark to Jerusalem, God's anger punishes suddenly and most severely, without warning, unrelated to our doing injustice, a person who acted from a good motivation:

> When they came to the threshing floor of Nakon, Uzzah reached out and took hold of the ark of God, because the oxen stumbled. God's anger burned against Uzzah because of his irreverent act; therefore, God struck him down, and he died there beside the ark of God. Then David was angry because God's wrath had broken out against Uzzah, and to this day that place is called Perez Uzzah.

Or what would Heschel do with this? King David takes a census of all the tribes. The prophet Gad tells David of God's displeasure at the taking of the census. Gad gives David a choice of punishments from which David chooses pestilence. And so: "The Lord sent a pestilence on Israel from that morning until the appointed time; and seventy thousands of the people died" (2 Samuel 24:15)

It is hard to see this as an act of a compassionate God, seeing that God does not say what was the sin in counting the people, the people who died had done no wrong, and it is hard to see the seventy thousand dead here as retribution for some human injustice. It was David who did the census; there was no warning; the people probably had no idea why they were dying; and a compassionate God would not have retaliated in such an extreme way.

Alas, the history of the two personae of the Jewish God is often a story like this, carefully selecting some sources to raise up for thought and life, while leaving other sources far in the background, to fend for themselves. With Heschel, this selectivity comes from his dedication to a compassionate, loving God of the Hebrew bible, the God he puts forward as appropriate for our worship, a neo-Hasidic God.

***

In effect, Heschel has neutralized PERSONA-E to a significant extent. God's self-transcendence is compromised by God's *presence* in a demonstrative, emotional divine life. God's judgmental side is *subsumed* under God's compassion, and God's anger is *righteous* anger only, and once again, driven by God's compassion. Thus does PERSONA-Y become victorious over PERSONA-E for this neo-Hasidic thinker. Finally, Heschel manages to recalculate what had been for the Hasidim a God of the Jews. Now, the God who was the *God of the Jews* is refurbished and moved en masse into an ethos for humankind, with a God of love and righteousness who has concern for every person there is, Greek or Jew, slave or free, woman or man.

8 The Holocaust and the God of the Jews

"The Holocaust" refers to the period between 1940–1945 when Nazi Germany and their accomplices murdered millions of Jews in Europe and elsewhere. Jews were shot to death in common graves, gassed to death in roving trucks, rounded up and stuffed into cattle cars to take them for hours to places like Auschwitz and Treblinka, where they were told they must shower to be ready to go to work for the Nazis. And they were told to make sure they knew where their clothes and shoes were. When the showers were turned on, no water came out. Instead, gas came rushing out to kill all. In the fields and forests of the countryside, Jews who had escaped the cities were hunted down and shot on the spot by the Nazi Gestapo. In the ghettoes of Europe, Jews were rounded up and confined to a small area from which they could not leave. Hunger, illness, and Nazi brutality murdered hundreds of thousands of Jews, while those who survived were broken in spirit and body. Such was the Warsaw ghetto with 400,000 Jews confined to an area of 3.4 square kilometers, where a quarter of a million Jews were sent away to death in 1942. Few Jews survived until the end of the war.

Where was the God of the Jews through all this? The Jews had suffered much through their history, but this was another dimension of suffering altogether. How could God stand by and let this happen? Was there really a God?

There developed a number of Jewish responses to this question. One response common among survivors and many other Jews was no longer to believe in God. Another was to be angry at God, as was my cousin Binyamin who had been a pious Jew until his time in brutal, forced labor, at Auschwitz. Still others affirmed that a human being could not possibly fathom God's ways and so nothing had changed. Some ultraorthodox Jews insist as well that no change in the concept of God was necessary, but that was because the murder of six million Jews was punishment . . . for the sins of Jews who were not ultra-orthodox.

Another was the theology of Richard Rubenstein, of the "Death of God," here meaning that there was no longer any interaction between God and the world, as evidenced by the Holocaust. (Rubenstein, 1992) Rubenstein had earlier argued vigorously that God could not have been omnipotent if the Holocaust occurred. (Rubenstein, 1968) Another is the theology of Rabbi Irving (Yitz) Greenberg who declared that: "No statement, theological or otherwise, should be made that would not be credible in the presence of burning children" (Greenberg, 1977: 23). Accordingly, Greenberg believed that in the Holocaust God had broken his covenant with the Jewish People, and that from now on the covenant could only be voluntary. (Greenberg, 1982).

But I am not here to give an inventory. I wish to focus on a unique and searing testimony that was written in real time by a pious Hassidic Rabbi and leader. This writing testified to his attempts to make sense of what was happening in Warsaw and the Warsaw ghetto. This is in the writing of Rabbi Kalonymous Kalman Shapiro (1889–1943), who came from the Polish town of Piaseczno and later moved to nearby Warsaw. The Nazis invaded Poland in September 1939. In late 1940 the rabbi, with all the Jews of Warsaw, were forced into the walled ghetto. There he ran a secret synagogue, hidden from the Nazis, and some of his writings are dated with the added, "written in hiding." His writings are from the time of the Nazi invasion in 1939 until his deportation from the ghetto in 1943, when the Jews were evacuated after an uprising against the Nazis. He was sent to the Nazi death camp of Miydanik to be murdered by the Nazis and dumped in a mass grave on November 3, 1943.

After the war, Polish workers clearing the debris of the destroyed Warsaw ghetto, found R. Shapiro's writings, including his sermons there in the ruins. They were published under the name *Esh Kodesh* (Pronounced "Aish Koedesh" – Holy Fire) in 1960, in Israel.

Nehemia Polen is the foremost researcher of R. Shapiro and *Esh Kodesh*. (See Polen, 1987, 253–269, 1994, and 1990, 30–33.) In his publications, Polen follows the changes in the rabbi's thinking on the horror of the atrocities to which he is daily witness, and as time goes on when the situation becomes less and less bearable.

Polen describes how in *Esh Kodesh*, in the first year of his writing, 1940, the rabbi assumed that the Jews were suffering from the Nazis because of Jewish sins. Polen then sees a change of direction by R. Shapiro starting in a sermon dated December 14, 1940, a direction maintained until the end. God could not possibly be punishing the Jews with such fury and abandon. Even for the Attribute of Judgment that was far from possible.

The horrors that he saw and heard of were of such an unimaginable magnitude that they could not possibly be God's punishment for our sins. The destruction was too enormous, too grotesque, too inflicting of human misery, to be explained in that way. Neither does R. Shapiro ever consider that the Jews were enduring the Talmudic "suffering of love." (If that were love, we could have lived without it.) The categories of Mercy and Judgment were not applicable anymore.

Tellingly, the rabbi does not consider applying the heavy curses in the Torah for unfaithfulness to God to the situation of the Jews in the ghetto. These curses are not so far from the Nazi actions on the Jews of Warsaw. "The Lord will plague you with diseases until he has destroyed you from the land you are entering to possess. The Lord will strike you with wasting disease, with fever and inflammation, with scorching heat and drought, with blight and mildew, which will plague you until you perish (Deuteronomy 28).

He could have seen these Torah curses as analogous to those being implemented by the Nazis. He does not. We can speculate that he could not think of his generation of Jews as so wicked as to deserve this as punishment. Or that the image of God the merciful was so dominant in his mind, as it was for the Hassidic movement of which he was part, that the possibility of such punishment could not be countenanced from God.

The final entries in *Esh Kodesh* from February–July 1942 turn to the theme of divine suffering, which we have seen advanced by some of the rabbis of the Talmud. Here Polen points to the entry of February 14, 1942. There Rabbi Shapiro writes that God's present suffering over his people is of an infinite magnitude, fitting for an infinite being. God's suffering is of such infinite power and anguish that it cannot be allowed to enter into the world, lest the world break apart entirely from not being able to contain such overwhelming suffering. So, God cannot act within the world now, for were he to do so, his anguish would destroy the world. So, God must go elsewhere to his "inner chambers," to suffer, in isolation from the world. Paradoxically, it is God's great love of the Jews that will not enable him to come to their rescue. God's mercy renders God vulnerable and unable to act.

Polen mentions prototypes for this sort of thinking in the rabbinic literature. Talmud Berakhot 29a, tells us that "When God remembers his children [the Jewish people] who dwell in misery among the nations of the world, He causes two tears to descend to the ocean and the sound is heard from one end of the world to the other." And in the Old Testament *Pseudepigrapha,* 3 Enoch: Chapter 48A, we find: "Then the right hand of the Omnipresent One wept, and five rivers of tears flowed from its five fingers, and, falling into the Great Sea, made the whole world quake" (see *Pseudepigrapha,* 1983, 301.) Thus R. Shapiro is enhancing an already existing motif in rabbinic literature.

Polen adds: "God is indeed not visible, but his occultation [concealment] is due not to callousness or indifference; rather it is a result of the depth and intensity," of his suffering" (Polen, 1994: 120). Paradoxically, it is because of God's infinite magnitude of love for the Jews that God cannot now engage within the world. If he were to do so, the world could not bear the infinite anguish and would collapse under the weight.

Yet, writes the rabbi:

> The one who pushes in and comes close to him ... weeps together with God. Just this makes the difference: the weeping, the pain, which a person undergoes by himself, alone, may have the effect of breaking him down ... But the weeping which a person does together with God – that strengthens him. He weeps – and is strengthened; he is broken – but finds courage. (Polen, 1994, 119.)

Rabbi Shapiro takes the divine suffering one step further in the next to last entry, July 11, 1942. Now, God's suffering and the suffering of the Jews change places. Until now it was God who is suffering the pain of the Jews. Now it becomes the Jews who are feeling God's own suffering, they are suffering along with him and for him. For now, God is the primary object of attack, the deep, metaphysical target of the enemy's hatred. In the depths of the Nazi hatred of the Jews is their hatred of the God of the Jews. Once again, God suffers a suffering so great that he must suffer and cry, alone, in his inner chambers. And the Jews, aye, the Jews, God's "chosen people," identify most closely with the divine anguish, and so they suffer the divine anguish. Our suffering is God's suffering transmuted into a finite, earthly form. Every Jew that dies now is suffering as a martyr for God's sake.

The Holocaust then is not an event solely inside human history. It is also an event of God's suffering and of the burden of his people suffering with him. The Holocaust is the ultimate mutuality of identity between God and his creation. Not in joy but in tormented anguish. Not a "justification" of the horrors have we here, only an attempt at a deeply sad understanding why it could not have been any other way.

For this pious Hasidic Rebbe, God is vulnerable, surprisingly, on account of his deep emotions. Heschel's theology of pathos turns around to bite both God and people. God cries, suffers, and grieves, which prevents God from interacting within the world, paradoxically because of his love of the world. So, in the final pages of this rabbi's sermons, *Esh Kodesh*, the suffering of the ghetto turns out to be a result of – *God's love*.

This "theodicy" may strike some as grotesque. I present it for you to features of this rabbi's thoughts under the severe duress of the brutal Nazi madness. Appreciate how this pious rabbi struggles beyond struggling to retain his life-long belief in and love of God, and to pass along the covenant of his people with God, despite it all. At the same time, he is not prepared to diminish in any way the horrific nature of the Warsaw events. He will not allow himself to understand it other than by giving it a metamystical/metaphysical grounding to make any sense of it.

In the end, the rabbi's God of the Holocaust is the old God of love and mercy, PERSONA-Y. In anguish and sadness, the rabbi continues to worship his God of Mercy.

9 Jewish Feminist Theology

Jewish feminist theology is the most significant and far-reaching theological development in Jewish thought in the past two hundred years since the rise of Hasidism and Reform Judaism. As a platform for radical transformation of Jewish thought, it stands in historical importance with previous radical transformations of the tradition.

In writing of Jewish feminist theology, I am not writing of a uniform school of thought. Jewish feminist theologians, as we will see, display various, though connected, theological positions. Feminist theology impacts Reform, Reconstructionist, Conservative, and Modern Orthodox Judaism to different degrees and in different ways. And, when writing of "women" and "women's experience" I am not referring to a unitary woman nor to a unitary experience. Yet, the basis of feminist discontent with extant religion and theology pretty much crosses categories and it is these feelings that I refer to as "women's experiences."

I limit myself to the relevance of feminist Jewish theology to the fate of the two personae of the Jewish God: PERSONA-Y and PERSONA-E. And also, in accordance with our topic, I limit myself to Jewish feminist theologians who engaged the Jewish tradition with the desire somehow to stay within Judaism, albeit with a reconfigured concept of God, religious language, and innovations in Jewish law.

The Problems of God

In the 1970s, Rita Gross was one to propose feminine language about God, "*in addition* to male forms" (Gross, 1979, 172). The introduction of female terms with regard to God would help reveal "all the links between male God language and the androcentric model of humanity, with its consequent eclipsing of women."

Judith Plaskow wrote this:

> The images we use to describe God, the qualities we attribute to God, draw on male pronouns and male experience and convey a sense of power and authority that is clearly male in character. The God at the surface of Jewish consciousness is a God with a voice of thunder, a God who as Lord and King rules his people and leads them into battle, a God who forgives like a father when we turn to him. (Plaskow, 2020, 228)

In this connection, consider this excerpt from 1 Chronicles: 29:10–12, included in the traditional daily liturgy:

> Blessed art thou, O Lord, the God of Israel our father, for ever and ever. Thine, O Lord, is the greatness, and the power, and the glory, and the victory, and the majesty; for all that is in the heavens and in the earth is thine; thine is the kingdom, O Lord, and thou art exalted as head above all. Both riches and honor come from thee, and thou rulest over all. In thy hand are power and might; and in thy hand it is to make great and to give strength to all. And now we thank thee, our God, and praise thy glorious name.

Elsewhere, Plaskow criticizes the male image of God, for God is "a dominating other . . . A great potentate fighting for his/her people and ruling over the world. (Plaskow, 1991, 138)

Plaskow links this patriarchal idea of God to the subordination of women in traditional Judaism: "God is a model of the many schemes of dominance that human beings create for themselves. As holy king he chooses the nation Israel as his holy people. As holy warrior he sanctions the destruction of peoples perceived as Other. As holy lawgiver he enacts the subordination of women in the Jewish community" (Plaskow, 1991, 132).

Accordingly, common to Jewish feminist theology is a rejection of a hierarchal God configured prominently as a male wielding dominating power *over* the world. Now, there are two ways to reject a hierarchal God configured prominently as a male wielding dominating power over the world. One way is to eliminate God's hierarchal position entirely in favor of an immanent God indwelling in the world. This replaces the God of Jewish patriarchal Otherness with a God internal to, and *empowering* us, men and women alike. This I will call "Feminist Immanence Theology," or just "Immanence Theology," for short. In the words of Mellissa Raphael: "Immanentism breaks down the traditional binary oppositions of spirit and flesh, heaven and earth, sacred and profane, where the value of one element in the duality – the transcendent – is secured at the expense of the other – the immanent" (Raphael, 1966, 23–24).

And here is how Marcia Falk puts it: "I hope to construct a theology of immanence that will both affirm the sanctity of the world and shatter the idolatrous reign of the lord/God/king" (Falk, 1989, 56–57).

A second way of rejecting a hierarchal God prominently configured as male wielding dominating power over the world is to *retain* God's hierarchal primacy while redefining the relationship between this God and the world, in terms other than power and domination. Let us call this view "Feminist Hierarchal Theology," or just "Hierarchal Theology," for short. Of the two, Immanence Theology is the major direction of Jewish feminist theology while the second has serious devotees as well. Both views, to repeat, reject a transcendent God who is prominently configured as a male wielding power over the world.

Both versions afford a new understanding from the ground up of God and of their relationship to us. On both views, the hierarchy of power has shaped the patriarchal social-political structure of male dominance to the great detriment of women. The traditional concept of God is an unjust concept of God and must be replaced or reconstructed to eliminate the patriarchal domination and repression of women.

We can see in both types of feminist theology, immanent and hierarchal, *in effect*, the collapse of the distinction between PERSONA-Y and PERSONA-E. That is because for Jewish feminist theology, as in feminist theology in general, the dominant images of God in the tradition fit most closely to the cluster of PERSONA-E. These images, on this view, tend to overshadow the passages and teachings in which God is depicted as kind and nurturing. But it's not only that PERSONA-E overshadows PERSONA-Y. It is more than that. The problem pertains internally to the very image of God *even* when kind and loving. And that is because God even then is seen as the mighty (male) King dispensing kindness to his subjects, essentially from the same position of power and dominance as PERSONA-E. This image preserves the male God who dominates the world with his mighty power, only this time being kind and loving. A God who personifies a male power can no longer serve as the God of the Jews. So goes the feminist reasoning. Plaskow says of the God of Jewish liturgy that God is "a king robed in majesty, a merciful but probing father, and master of the world (Plaskow, 1991, 129). Kind at times, yes, but even then, probing, a father, a master.

Jewish Feminist Immanence Theology

Jewish feminist theology came to full life in the early 1970s, with Judith Plaskow's *Standing Again at Sinai*, the first authored book dedicated to the subject. Plaskow was and remains a central figure in Jewish feminist theology.

Quickly the genie's bottle opened, and Jewish feminist theology began to flourish. Early on, Plaskow described being torn between the "deeply androcentric Judaism in which I was raised, and the excitement and new possibilities opened up by my experiences of feminist community" (Christ and Plaskow, 2016, 116. The quotation is from Plaskow.)

Plaskow's Jewish identity and sense of Jewish community were too important to her and so she set about to create a feminist revision of People, Torah, and God. Traditional texts for Plaskow are to be honored but are not a final authority, being only a basis for reconstruction. Speaking of Jewish women, Plaskow writes: "The Bible is very much our Bible" (Plaskow, 1976, 4).

Plaskow insists on the primacy of Jewish feminist theology in the landscape of Jewish feminism (Plaskow, 2020). Jewish feminists who devote themselves only to gaining equal "civil rights" for women in Jewish law are treating the symptoms and not the basis of the problem. The paradigmatic Jew remains the male Jew. (Just think of Annie in "Annie Get Your Gun," singing to a man, "Anything you can do I can do better!") The root cause of womens' Otherness is theological, for Plaskow, because of the way the tradition speaks of and images God, as a dominant male.

I let Plaskow speak for herself in what God is for her:

> I believe in a God who is present in everything and yet at the same time is not identical with all that is. Just as a community may be more than the sum of its parts, so God is more than the totality of creation and includes and unifies creation. The idea of unity or oneness is particularly central to my understanding of God. To me, believing in God means affirming that, despite the fractured, scattered, and conflicted nature of our experience of both the world and ourselves, there is a unity that embraces and contains our diversity and that connects all things to each other (Christ and Plaskow, 2016, 184. The quotation is from Plaskow).

And this is what Plaskow means by "monotheism": Monotheism for her means that God encompasses a unitary everything.

So, Plaskow urges adopting metaphors in which God is experienced in nature and is present in an empowered community. And Plaskow favors anthropomorphic language for its ability to reach emotions inaccessible to abstract language, while rejecting all metaphors of domination. Yet, she is very clear when saying that, "I do not think of God in personal terms, and I prefer not to use any personal language to describe or address God (Christ and Plaskow, 2016, 230. The quotation is from Plaskow). For Plaskow, anthropomorphic expressions might be useful in our daily language about God, but "beneath" them they denote the creative source of all beings.

This feminist understanding undercuts the distinction between PERSONA-Y and PERSONA-E, for both are male gods who act from a position of great power. Even though PERSONA-Y may be *more* immanent than PERSONA-E, PERSONA-Y nevertheless remains unacceptable as an Otherness predominantly exercising "power-over."

Hierarchical Jewish Feminist Theology

Hierarchal Jewish Feminist Theology is less central in Jewish feminist theology than what we have seen until now. It too rejects a hierarchal God whose significant image is of a male king employing power over his domain. But it does so not by rejecting divine hierarchal primacy but by revising the role of the hierarchal God's relationship to the world. The leading Jewish feminist voice here is perhaps that of Rachel Adler, who declares in a manifesto-like way that: "For me, the otherness of God is compellingly real and infinitely precious. Eradicating otherness, breaking down all boundaries, between self and other, self and God, God and world, simultaneously eradicates relatedness" (Adler, 1998, 91).

Adler rejects the idea that disparities of power and authority are inherently oppressive, naming relationships of disparity that do not "require disadvantaging or degrading the less powerful or less authoritative participant." These include where one has special competence and helps another in need, helping another to acquire a skill, or self-understanding, or spiritual illumination. These can be relationships in which recipients are made partners, to benefit and empower (Adler, 1998, 94).

For Adler, this is precisely the relationship between God and us. God is "the experienced helper" showing us "to ourselves as attainers of competence." For Adler, "God is the primary Otherness in a world where, as Emmanuel Levinas teaches, self constantly raises its face to the other." And, "We and God are interdependent, friends, lovers, and co-creators of the world." (Adler, 1998, 93) "To continue to affirm that we are in relationship with this God is not to affirm God-as-power or God-as-patterner in some abstract sense, but rather to assert that we as actors have moral weight: we matter to God" (Adler, 1998, 95).

For these reasons, Adler disagrees about thinking of God theologically only in neuter terminology, this against the position endorsed by Plaskow. Personal anthropomorphic language is necessary to capture the personal nature of our mutuality with God. We have to create feminine images of God alongside the male ones to avoid falling into the maleness of God.

Adler thus preserves a hierarchal relationship between God and us but not a hierarchy of power-over. God is the primary Other who "creates and upholds the distinctness of all things one from another." This is clearly a God standing at the apex of a world hierarchy. However, this time God is a partner with us in the world, an "experienced helper."

The Israeli Jewish feminist theologian, Tamar Ross, has on occasion expressed (a bit tentatively with "maybe") a somewhat similar position to that of Rachel Adler about our images of God (Ross, 2004). Ross is in favor of what she calls "the selective preservation of some vestiges, at least, of gender distinctions."

Ross has written of "The intrinsic value of hierarchic theological conceptions" (Ross, 2004, 135, see also Ross, 2007, 222). These include, that God as outside of us may be necessary for prayer, the notion of divine providence may be crucial to the development of morality, and a God who is over creation may be important "in imaging a God who is more than the projection of our subjective desires." Ross has also argued for a measure of continuity with the age-old Jewish tradition and the constitutive role a hierarchal God plays in the spiritual life of devotees. Yet, with regard to revelation, Ross maintains a God immanent in history.

As we have seen before in other cases, these positions in feminist Jewish theology select some strands of the tradition to address while ignoring others. Feminists might have found other rich sources to address, as for example in some themes of the Hasidic writings, or as does Tamar Ross who mines the writings of Rabbi Abraham Isaac Kook for feminist-friendly theological bedrock. In the case of feminism, what determines the selectivity is the anguish of feminist women over their marginalized place within the tradition and in their marginalized part in the historical development of that tradition. This includes the ramifications of the tradition for male–female relations in the flesh. So, this selectivity takes its place with others in the long story of God and the Jewish people.

∗∗∗

This brings me to the end of my story, for now. This has been a sketch of part of a massive literature over the ages in which the God of the Jews found in the Hebrew Bible challenged the religious and moral sensibilities of selected Jewish thinkers. This challenge arises differently in different ages and is a symptom of an ongoing intricate dance consisting of the Jews trying to understand their God. We Jews must keep adding to the story.

References

Adler, R. (1998). *Engendering Judaism, an Inclusive Theology and Ethics*. Boston: Beacon Press.

Bareli, M. and Kellner, M. (2021). Maimonides on the status of Judaism. In Sadiq, S. and Krinis, E. (Eds.), *Cultural Encounters in Late Antiquity and the Middle Ages: Studies in Honour of Daniel J. Lasker*. Berlin: DeGruyter.

Ben-Sasson, H. (2018). *Understanding YHWH, The Name of God in Biblical, Rabbinic and Medieval Jewish Thought*. New York: Palgrave Macmillan.

Ben-Sasson, H. and Halbertal, M. (n.d.). The name 'YHWH' and the Attribute of Mercy. (Hebrew). In Nihof, M., Maroz, R. and Yehonatan G. (Eds.), *V'Zot L'Yehuda*. Jerusalem: Mosad Bialik and Institute of Jewish Studies, Hebrew University.

Bergman, S. H. (1991). *Dialogical Philosophy from Kierkegaard to Rosenzweig*. Albany, NY: Suny Press.

Christ, C. P. and Plaskow, J. (2016). *Goddess and God in the World: Conversations in Embodied Theology*. Minneapolis, MN: Fortress Press.

Cohen, H. (1972). *The Religion of Reason Out of the Sources of Judaism*. New York: Fredrich Unger Publishing.

Dresner, S. (1974). *Levi Yitzhak of Berditchev: Portrait of a Hasiduic Master*. New York: Hartmore House.

Falk, M. (1989). Toward a feminist Jewish reconstruction of monotheism, *Tikkun*, 4, 53–56.

Furnal, J. (2016). Abraham Joshua Heschel and *Nostra Aetate*: Shaping the Catholic reconsideration of Judaism during Vatican II, *Religions*, 7(6).

Gellman, J. (1994). *The Fear, the Trembling, and The Fire: Kierkegaard and Hasidic Masters on the Binding of Isaac*. Lanham, MD: University Press of America.

Greenberg, I. (1977). *Auschwitz: Beginning of a New Era? Reflections on the Holocaust*. New York: Ktav Publishing.

Greenberg, I. (1982). *Voluntary Covenant*. New York: National Jewish Resource Center.

Gross, R. M. (1979). Female God language in a Jewish context. In Christ, C. P. and Plaskow, J. (Eds.), *Womanspirit Rising*. San Francisco: Harper.

Halevi, J. (2008). The Song of the Distant Dove, Scheindlin, R. P. (Trans.). *The Song of the Distant Dove: Judah Halevi's Pilgrimage*. Oxford: Oxford University Press.

Heschel, A. J. (1944). Reason and revelation in Saadia's philosophy, *The Jewish Quarterly Review*, New Series, 34(4), 391–408.

Heschel, A. J. (1951). *Man Is Not Alone*. New York: Jewish Publication Society.

Heschel, A. J. (1955). *The Prophets*. Philadelphia: The Jewish Publication Society of America.

Heschel, A. J. (1959). *God in Search of Man, A Philosophy of Judaism*. New York: Meridian Books and the Jewish Publication Society.

Heschel, A.J. (2021) Heavenly Torah as Refracted through the Generations. Hebrew. Jerusalem: Magid Books, Koren Publications.

Heschel, A. J. (1966). No religion is an island, *Union Theological Quarterly Review*, 21, 1–22.

Idel, M. (1988). *Kabbalah: New Perspectives*. New Haven, CT: Yale University Press.

Lasker, D. J. (2022). *Karaism: An Introduction to the Oldest Surviving Alternative Judaism*. Liverpool: Liverpool University Press; The Littman Library of Jewish Civilization.

Maimonides. (1963). *Guide of the Perplexed*, Pines, S. (Trans.). Chicago: Chicago University Press.

Matt, D. C. (2009). *The Essential Kabbalah*. New York: HarperCollins.

D. C. Matt, (2018) Translator, The Zohar, Pritzker Edition, Stanford: Stanford University Press.

Menahem Azariah da Fano. (1999/2000). "The Mother of all Living." (Hebrew). *The Book of Ten Declarations*. (Hebrew). Jerusalem: Yismach Lev Publishing.

Polen, N. (1987). Divine weeping: Rabbi Kalonymous Shapiro's Theology of Catastrophe in the Warsaw ghetto, *Modern Judaism*, 7, 253–269.

Polen, N. (1994). *The Holy Fire, The Teachings of Rabbi Kalonymous Kalman Shapira, the Rebbe of the Warsaw Ghetto*. Lanham, MA: Rownam & Littlefield.

Polen, N. (1990). Sensitization to Holiness: The life and works of Rabbi Kalonymous Kalmish Shapiro," *Jewish Action*, 50, 30–33.

Poma, A. (1997). *The Critical Philosophy of Herman Cohen*, Denton, J (Trans.). Albany, NJ: SUNY Press.

Plaskow, J. (1991). *Standing Again at Sinai; Judaism from a Feminist Perspective*. San Francisco: HarperCollins.

Plaskow, J. (1976). The Jewish feminist: Conflict in identities. In Koltun, E. (Ed.), *The Jewish Woman: New Perspectives*. New York: Schocken Books.

Plaskow, J. (2020). The right question is theological. In Heschel, S. (Ed.), *On Being a Jewish Feminist*. New York: Schocken Books.

Pseudipigrapha. (1983). Trans. Alexander, P. In Charlesworth, J. H. (Ed.), *The Old Testament Pseudipigrapha*. Yale: Yale University Press.

Raphael, M. (1996). *Thealogy and Embodiment, The Post-Patriarchal Reconstruction of Female Sacrality.* Sheffield, UK: Sheffield Academic Press.

Rapoport-Albert, A. and and Kwasman, T. (2006). Late Aramaic: The literary and linguistic context of the *Zohar. Aramaic Studies*, 4(1), 5–19.

Rosenzweig, F. (1998). *God, Man and World: Lectures and Essays by Franz Rosenzweig.* Galli, B. E. (Ed. and Trans.). Syracuse, NY: Syracuse University Press.

Rosenzweig, F. (2005). *Star of Redemption.* Galli B. E. (Trans.). Madison: University of Wisconsin Press.

Ross, T. (2004). *Expanding the Palace of Torah, Orthodoxy and Feminism.* Waltham, MA: Brandeis University Press.

Ross, T. and Plaskow, J. (2007). The view from here: Gender theory and gendered realities: An exchange between Tamar Ross and Judith Plaskow. In *Nashim: A Journal of Jewish Women's Studies & Gender Issues*, 13(1), 207–251.

Rubenstein, R. (1992). *After Auschwitz: History, Theology, and Contemporary Judaism.* Baltimore: Johns Hopkins University Press.

Rubenstein, R. (1968). God's omnipotence in Rabbinic Judaism. In *The Religious Imagination: A Study in Psychoanalysis and Jewish Theology.* Boston: University Press of America.

Saadia Gaon. (1948). *The Book of Beliefs and Opinions.* Rosenblatt S. (Trans). New Haven: Yale University Press.

Scholem, G. (1995). *Major Trends in Jewish Mysticism.* New York: Schocken Books.

Stump, E. (1997). Saadia Gaon on the problem of evil. *Faith and Philosophy*, 14, 523–549.

Turner, Y. (2014a). Sacrifice and repentance: The religious thought of Herman Cohen, Franz Rosenzweig and Joseph B. Soloveitchik. In Houtman, G., Poorhuis, M., Schwartz, J. and Turner, Y. (Eds.). *The Actuality of Sacrifice – Past and Present*, Leiden and Boston: Brill Publishing.

Turner, Y. (2014b). Prayer and love in Franz Rosenzweig's *Star of Redemption, European Journal of Jewish Studies*, 8(2), 173–193.

Urbach, E. E. (1975). *The Sages, Their Concepts and Beliefs*, Jerusalem: Magnes Press.

Wolfson, E. (1995). *Along the Path: Studies in Kabbalistic Hermeneutics, Myth, and Symbolism*, Albany; SUNY Press.

Zohar, The Book of (2018). *Pritzker Edition*, 12 volumes, Daniel C. Matt, (Trans.). Palo Alto: Stanford University Press.

Acknowledgments

I thank: Michael Peterson, editor of this Elements series; the Van Leer Institute where I am a library Fellow, where I wrote much of this Element; Jonathan Malino who read parts of the manuscript and gave excellent advice; Yossi Turner who early on gave very good suggestions on how to conceive of this Element and for his part in the writing of this Element; Menachem Kellner who was helpful on Medieval Jewish theology; Ronit Irshay, Charlotte Katzoff, and Tamar Ross who read and commented on Feminist Jewish Theology; Cass Fisher, who was helpful both in content and as a cheer-leader; Uriel Gellman who was helpful with sources from the Hasidić literature; and my revered Reform Christian teacher, Alvin Plantinga.

Cambridge Elements ≡

The Problems of God

Series Editor
Michael L. Peterson
Asbury Theological Seminary

Michael L. Peterson is Professor of Philosophy at Asbury Theological Seminary. He is the author of *God and Evil* (Routledge); *Monotheism, Suffering, and Evil* (Cambridge University Press); *With All Your Mind* (University of Notre Dame Press); *C. S. Lewis and the Christian Worldview* (Oxford University Press); *Evil and the Christian God* (Baker Book House); and *Philosophy of Education: Issues and Options* (Intervarsity Press). He is co-author of *Reason and Religious Belief* (Oxford University Press); *Science, Evolution, and Religion: A Debate about Atheism and Theism* (Oxford University Press); and *Biology, Religion, and Philosophy* (Cambridge University Press). He is editor of *The Problem of Evil: Selected Readings* (University of Notre Dame Press). He is co-editor of *Philosophy of Religion: Selected Readings* (Oxford University Press) and *Contemporary Debates in Philosophy of Religion* (Wiley-Blackwell). He served as General Editor of the Blackwell monograph series Exploring Philosophy of Religion and is founding Managing Editor of the journal *Faith and Philosophy*.

About the Series
This series explores problems related to God, such as the human quest for God or gods, contemplation of God, and critique and rejection of God. Concise, authoritative volumes in this series will reflect the methods of a variety of disciplines, including philosophy of religion, theology, religious studies, and sociology.

Cambridge Elements $\equiv$

The Problems of God

Elements in the Series

A full series listing is available at: www.cambridge.org/EPOG

Printed in the United States
by Baker & Taylor Publisher Services